Ultimate Basic Business Skills

Training an Effective Workforce

ASTD Ultimate Series

CHRISTEE GABOUR ATWOOD

ASTD
PRESS

Alexandria, Virginia

ASTD Press is an internationally renowned source of insightful and practical information on workplace learning and performance topics, including training basics, evaluation and return on investment, instructional systems development, e-learning, leadership, and career development.

Ordering information: Books published by ASTD Press can be purchased by visiting our website at store.astd.org or by calling 800.628.2783 or 703.683.8100.

Library of Congress Control Number: 2008937407

ISBN-10: 1-56286-589-7
ISBN-13: 978-1-56286-589-4

ASTD Press Editorial Staff:
Director: Dean Smith
Manager, ASTD Press: Jacqueline Edlund-Braun
Senior Associate Editor: Tora Estep
Senior Associate Editor: Justin Brusino
Editorial Assistant: Victoria Devaux
Full-Service Design, Development, and Production: Aptara Inc., Falls Church, VA, www.aptaracorp.com
    Development/Production Editor: Robin C. Bonner
    Copyeditor: Ellen N. Feinstein
    Indexer: Kidd Indexing
    Proofreader: Sarah A. Bonner
    Interior Design: Lisa Adamitis
Cover Design: Ana Ilieva Foreman
Cover Illustration: Shutterstock.com

Printed by Versa Press, Inc., East Peoria, Illinois, www.versapress.com

The ASTD Ultimate Series

ASTD Press's *Ultimate* series is a natural follow-on to the popular *Trainer's WorkShop* series. Like the *Trainer's WorkShop* series, the *Ultimate* series is designed to be a one-stop, practical, hands-on road map that helps you quickly develop training programs. Each book in the *Ultimate* series offers a full range of practical tools you can apply or adapt to a variety of training scenarios. As in the *Trainer's WorkShop* series, you will find exercises, handouts, assessments, structured experiences, and ready-to-use presentations, along with detailed facilitation instructions. So what's the difference? The *Ultimate* series aims to present the full scope of various topics, offering today's overcommitted training professionals even MORE practical and scalable help: More practical exercises, handouts, assessments, and other ready-to-deploy training solutions. More detailed instructions. Broader topic coverage. More downloadable material. In short, more value for your training budget dollars.

Table of Contents

Preface

This publication can be described as a "training department in a book." It offers ready-to-present programs for some of the most valuable professional skills that the members of an organization can learn. It creates a foundation of courses for the organization's training department, which frees learning professionals to concentrate their efforts on the current challenges specific to their organizations but to still offer a core curriculum of programs that address the ongoing needs of their workforce.

Ultimate Basic Business Skills: Training an Effective Workforce focuses on the skills needed by every individual in an organization. The chapters on customer service skills offer development programs to help not only in serving and creating loyal customers, but also in partnering with internal customers to create a stronger team. The section on interpersonal skills addresses those practices that allow the organization's members to communicate more effectively and thereby reduce the misunderstandings that can occur in interactions between different personalities and backgrounds. The business skills chapters offer training to enhance organizational abilities and improve business documentation and processes. The section on professionalism equips participants to present a positive image and to practice the behaviors that represent a strong and focused member of the business world.

Each of the five sections contains complete modules—with all materials needed for facilitation. Each module is designed as a half-day session but includes notes and optional activities to allow expansion to a longer session, if desired. The separate modules can also be blended to provide specialized workshops tailored to an organization's specific needs.

The half-day training sessions are excerpted from or based on other books from ASTD Press— and therefore draw on the expertise of the outstanding authors of ASTD Press. I've added, updated, and modified this material from my own perspective as an experienced trainer. Each module notes the ASTD publications from which its materials are excerpted, so learning professionals can refer to those volumes to develop more in-depth understanding and training programs on any of the topics presented in this book.

This book is designed to help learning professionals offer a variety of business skills to all individuals in their organizations. The need for these types of professional skills is not restricted to any single department. For example, the skills that help customer service representatives develop and maintain loyal customers can also be valuable to others in the organization who will never encounter an external customer. That's because those same interpersonal skills can be applied to dealings with co-workers and other business partners. Likewise, the organizational skills that help project managers complete their work on deadline and achieve quality outcomes can also help supervisors ensure the successful completion of tasks in their departments. Moreover, everyone in the organization uses communication skills during every interaction with co-workers, vendors, and members of the community.

As part of the *Ultimate* series, *Ultimate Basic Business Skills: Training an Effective Workforce* serves the mission of these books by creating a well-rounded training department in volumes that learning professionals can use to expand their training offerings immediately and answer the needs of organizations to compete in the global workplace.

In the words of President John F. Kennedy, "Leadership and learning are indispensable to each other." *Ultimate Basic Business Skills* strives to create the learning opportunities that will develop the leaders of tomorrow's workforce.

Christee Gabour Atwood
Alexandria, Louisiana
October 2009

Section One:
Getting Started

How to Use This Book 1

What's in This Chapter?

- Discussion of the benefits of business skills training

- Explanation of how to use this book for best results

- Description of what's in this workbook and the accompanying CD

▲   ▲   ▲

Why Business Skills Training?

What makes a business successful? We can include outstanding products, valuable services, sound business practices, financial acumen, a solid reputation, and the list goes on.

All these standards of success have one element in common: people. An individual in the workforce creates, produces, and improves those outstanding products. An employee delivers that valuable service and generates loyalty by meeting and exceeding customer needs. Individual leaders in the organization design and enforce those sound business practices. Financial acumen arises from years of those individuals' experiences and their ability to continue to build on that foundation. The company's solid reputation emerges as a result of the daily activities of those employees.

Organizations that want to continue this pattern of growth are wise to invest in those individuals. Past experience has shown us that training increases not only employees' knowledge, but also their job satisfaction, and this translates into the improved retention rates that benefit organizational success. Moreover, training in business skills creates the foundation for those employees to advance to new roles in the organization.

Business skills encompass a wide range of competencies, and the programs presented in this book offer the groundwork to enhance those proficiencies. Future volumes will allow more specialized training to address the evolving needs of the workforce.

How Can These Workshops Help?

The individuals in a company create its knowledge base and continue to build on that base as they learn lessons, share best practices, and adapt procedures to incorporate their new knowledge. Organizations increase the productivity and the satisfaction level of these individuals by introducing them to improved methods of communication, customer interaction, personal management, and other valuable business skills.

Improved employee practices, increased retention, and a continued commitment to build on current knowledge all help to strengthen organizations' practices. Those practices include the success factors we mentioned earlier: product development, outstanding service, sound business practices, financial acumen, and reputable standing in the business world.

Who Needs These Courses?

These courses represent a sound investment for individuals at all levels of development in the organization. Forward-thinking organizations have discovered that the time for career planning is as soon as a new employee joins their ranks. They have also discovered that training and development should begin at the same time.

Ideally, these courses will include individuals from all areas of the organization so they can develop networks beyond their departments as they learn the materials offered in the sessions. Although these courses are not expected to be cures for performance problems, they are designed to work in conjunction with performance management and coaching procedures to help struggling employees improve.

How to Use This Workbook

Whether you're an experienced facilitator or a novice instructor, you'll find that this workbook is a useful resource to develop and facilitate workshops on business skills. You can substitute exercises or segments to customize the programs to meet the specific needs of your audiences. This book is not intended to be read cover to cover; rather, the workshops should be implemented as needed.

Here are the training materials included in this book and on the accompanying CD:

- guidelines to design your business skills workshops

- materials and instructions to facilitate your training sessions

- tools to evaluate the workshops

- training workshop formats and agendas that incorporate a range of training activities. (You can use these exactly as they appear in the book or modify them to suit your organization's need and your facilitation style.)

- learning activities, tools, and assessments designed to support the workshops

- Microsoft PowerPoint presentations to accompany each workshop format. You'll find thumbnails of the slides at the ends of the chapters in which they are referenced. The CD also contains color versions of the slides that can be printed three-to-a-page and used as class handouts.

All assessments, instruments, and tools can be found on the CD. Copy them in advance to create packets for each attendee. You'll distribute the rest of the handouts and tools at appropriate times during the workshop.

Here are some suggestions to help you use this book effectively:

- *Skim the book.* Browse the table of contents of this workbook. Study the lists in the **What's in This Chapter** sections. Get an overall sense of the layout and structure of the information included.

- *Be sure you understand the concepts of basic business skills.* To study the overview of business skills, review the chapters that introduce each category. Chapter 3 gives the overview of customer service skills, and chapter 8 explains the content of the courses that comprise the section on interpersonal skills. Review chapter 13 to understand basic business skills. An overview of professionalism is offered in chapter 18. In addition, you can consult some of the resources listed at the end of each workshop chapter to find additional information and programs that offer extended training on any of the included topics.

- *Assess the benefits of improved business skills for your organization.* Take the time to consider the benefits of business skills training and how that could advance your organization's goals. For example, imagine how efficiency could be improved if members of the workforce practiced effective time management and project management techniques. Consider how employee collaboration could be enhanced through effective communication skills and evaluate how a higher level of professionalism could affect your organization's image and reputation.

- *Review the methods to present a high-impact program.* Chapter 2 outlines ideas to make your program successful. You'll learn techniques to help attendees become more comfortable as they participate in the activities and practice sessions during the course of the workshop. You can set an example for attendees as you model the collaboration and communication behaviors you want them to develop.

- *Study the sample program agendas.* Review the agendas for the sessions to decide which format will address and satisfy your group's specific needs. Go through each agenda, even if you don't plan to present all of the workshops at this time. You may discover an exercise in one agenda that isn't included in the format you plan to use but that would be a great benefit to your specific participants. Just replace an exercise in the agenda you're using with one from the other programs. The time listings on each activity will help you make replacements and adjust the schedule to fit your desired workshop length.

- *Customize your training program.* Because this workbook includes everything you need for a workshop, you can use your time to make the program your own instead of creating agendas and formulating exercises. Mold it and incorporate your own personality to make the presentation suit your style. When the program fits you, you'll get more pleasure from your presentation, and you'll communicate the concepts to your learners more effectively.

What's on the CD?

All assessments, tools, training instruments, and PowerPoint slides used in this workbook are included on the accompanying CD. Follow the instructions in the appendix, "Using the Accompanying Compact Disc," at the end of the workbook, or read "How to Use This CD" on the CD itself.

Icons

For easy reference and to help you quickly locate specific materials and tools for training design and instructions, icons are included in the margins throughout this workbook and in the learning activities. Here are the icons and what they represent:

 Assessment: Appears when an agenda or learning activity includes an assessment.

 CD: Indicates materials included on the CD accompanying this workbook.

 Clock: Indicates suggested timeframes for an activity.

 Instructions: Identifies step-by-step instructions for completing the learning activity.

 Learning Activity: Indicates a structured exercise for use in a training session.

 Materials: Indicates what is required to conduct the session.

 Objectives: Identifies training goals for developing skills during that particular session.

 PowerPoint Slide: Indicates PowerPoint presentations and individual slides.

 Tool: Identifies an item that offers information that participants will find useful in the training session and on the job.

 Training Instrument: Indicates interactive training materials for participant use.

 What to Do Next: Denotes recommendations for what to do after you have completed a particular section of the workbook.

In the next chapter, we will discuss workshop preparations to ensure that you will have sufficient time to set up the room and prepare the participant materials. In addition, you will find instructions for preparing participant materials for each workshop as well as an explanation of the principles of effective facilitation.

What to Do Next

- Study the contents of the workbook to familiarize yourself with the material it offers.

- Complete the assessments in the workbook to rate your own business skills and to determine your areas for development.

- Review the contents of the CD and open some of the items, so you understand how the materials are organized and accessed.

Facilitating Business Skills Training

2

What's in This Chapter?

- Overview of workshop preparations
- Instructions for preparing participant materials
- Explanation of the principles of effective facilitation

These programs are designed to be discovery sessions. Instead of teaching and lecturing, facilitators guide learners through interactive experiences and discussions that allow them to come to their own realizations. Learners also have opportunities to learn from each other and to gather information from the course materials.

No two sessions are ever exactly alike, which is an exciting feature of these workshops. As you grow and learn from past workshops, these added insights will enhance your classes. Moreover, some groups will focus on the areas of the curriculum in which they need the most assistance. As you become more comfortable with the material, you'll be flexible enough to address those areas and still effectively cover the other materials of the course.

To ensure success, the first step is to create the right environment for an interactive session.

Establishing a Learning Environment

These workshops are not lecture sessions, so the room setup should allow for interaction and movement between the tables.

The sessions include writing, group presentations, and small group activities and discussions. The optimal seating arrangement for a group of 15 or more is a chevron shape: an angled classroom-style arrangement with tables arranged in a V-formation.

Learners can sit at the tables and take notes, and the angled arrangement lets participants see each other and interact. An alley down the center and space between the tables allows you to walk around and monitor progress during the learning activities.

If space isn't sufficient for chevron-style seating, classroom seating (rows of tables and chairs) is a good alternative. Theatre seating (rows of chairs without tables) is not an option for these sessions because the learners will have many opportunities to write and will need desks.

For a group of fewer than 15 attendees, a U-shape layout is an excellent option. This allows maximum interaction among the participants and permits the facilitator to move to any learner's location easily.

Refer to the list of materials at the beginning of each module to gather all the necessary items to produce any of the sessions listed in this workbook. Additional materials can help make sessions even more effective. For example, an assortment of small toys on the workshop tables gives kinesthetic learners something to occupy their hands, which aids their concentration. These might include peg games, stress balls, and assorted dexterity puzzles.

Posters, colorful flipchart signs, decorations, or items that support workshop themes can add a playful element to your workshop environment. In addition, participants who are auditory learners will enjoy listening to music when they enter and during the learning activities; this can reduce the stress that accumulates in a room that's too quiet.

Workshop Preparations

Try to set up your room the day before the session begins. This will enable you to deal with any problems caused by missing or faulty equipment, and it will ensure that you're not worn out from moving tables and equipment when your attendees arrive.

Room Setup Checklist

☐ Set a facilitator table at the head of the room with your instructor's guide, timer for exercises, and attendee handouts.

☐ Load your CD or MP3 player with suitable music.

☐ Turn on your computer with the Microsoft PowerPoint presentation loaded directly onto the hard drive. Don't play the PowerPoint slides from the CD because that slows down the response time and offers more chances for malfunction.

☐ Use a remote control to advance the slides of your PowerPoint presentation so you are not forced to stand at the front of the room for the entire program. Ensure that your device works and has fresh batteries.

☐ Provide basic items for your own convenience, including a glass of water, mints, headache remedies, and tissues. Your facilitator table should have any other items you think you'll need.

☐ Check all markers to make sure they have ink.

☐ Estimate the number of flipchart pages you'll use in your session, and see that you have enough on your pad.

☐ Practice writing on the flipchart to ensure that the easel is stable.

☐ Check the ink supply if you're using dry-erase markers, and make sure you know the difference between the dry erase and the flipchart markers.

☐ Use flipchart pages with temporary adhesive on the back, or tear pieces of masking tape into shorts strips and attach them to the back of the flipchart easel, so you can quickly post pages around the room.

☐ Give out prizes from your local dollar store: A prize bag is an optional item that's always a big hit. It can be a fun incentive to get attendees into the spirit of competition.

☐ Check to see if there's a phone in the room. If so, turn off the ringer for the duration of the workshop.

☐ Learn how to operate the thermostat.

☐ Locate the light switches.

☐ Ask about fire exits and restroom locations if you are in an unfamiliar building.

☐ Ensure that the room is set for the appropriate number of attendees.

☐ Take time to sit down in the back row, as well as various seats around the outer edges of the tables, to confirm that everyone will have a good view of the screen and of all activity at the front of the room.

☐ Post signs, posters, or any theme decorations.

☐ Post the agenda, rules of conduct, room locators, or any other materials you've created for the session.

☐ Post a flipchart page titled "Parking Lot," to be used when learners have questions that are not directly related to the current section of the class. They can attach sticky notes with their questions so you can address them later in the session or during the summary.

☐ Prepare the site for your attendees once you feel confident that you've addressed all the details of your meeting room.

Participant Materials

Put these materials at each attendee's place:

• handouts and extra paper for notes

• a few sticky notes attached to the front of each set of handouts

• pencils or pens

- a name badge (don't use table tents because your learners move around during these interactive workshops).

Place these materials on each table for group use:

- markers for activities on flipcharts and to write on name badges

- a few flipchart pages

- snacks, mints, and candies (optional)

- table toys (optional).

Principles of Effective Facilitation

Once you've set the stage, you're ready to focus on facilitation techniques. Here are some best practices to help guarantee the success of your session:

- *Introduce yourself and briefly visit with individuals as they enter the room.* This immediately begins to reduce participant stress levels and dissipates some of that nervous energy you'll probably have at the beginning of the session.

- *Set ground rules at the beginning of the session.* Sample ground rules are listed in each of the chapters.

- *Use verbal and nonverbal reinforcement techniques to create rapport.* Nod your head, make eye contact, avoid negative words such as *but* and *wrong*, smile, and show appreciation for participation to reduce learner anxiety and create a comfortable atmosphere.

- *Watch for nonverbal cues.* Are they fidgeting? Do they look confused? Is anyone dozing off? Are people putting on sweaters? Respond as needed to the cues you receive.

- *Use appropriate humor as a communication tool, but it's not necessary to tell jokes.* We are not all meant to be stand-up comedians. Stories and personal experiences are often the best humor you can use in training sessions.

- *Keep lecture time to a minimum.* If you find that a segment of the workshop does not elicit enough discussion, modify the format to let the participants teach that section. Remember, it's your workshop: You make the rules.

- *Consider awarding certificates to graduates.* A certificate reinforces the participants' feelings of accomplishment. In addition, participants will probably hang the certificate in their cubicles, where it will be seen much more often than a flyer from the training department. In this way, certificates become advertisements for your future training programs.

- *Count to eight after you ask a question.* One of the big challenges for facilitators is to let a moment of silence pass. Just remember that the participants don't know this material as well as you do. It takes them a little longer to process the new information, make connections, and respond to your queries.

- *Check frequently for understanding.* Ask your learners to summarize the main points of the material you presented, and ask if they understand the topic.

- *Tailor your delivery to your audience.* You may discover that members of your group are sports enthusiasts. That's an opportunity to pull out your best sports analogies. Current news may be foremost in everyone's minds. Adapt your material to include the latest developments. Consider the level of education and expertise in your group, and drop the acronyms and buzzwords to ensure that everyone understands the message you're trying to communicate.

- *Handle distractions calmly.* Acknowledge and immediately move the focus to problem solving. Ensure that your actions are diplomatic and do not demean the individuals involved.

- *Take a break and privately discuss the situation with the disruptive participant if problem behavior persists.* Remember, yours is the final word. You have the right to define the limits of acceptable behavior and to ask a person who is going beyond those limits to leave the workshop.

- *Incorporate words that appeal to the different learning styles.* For your visual learners, use phrases like, "Let's take a look at this." Auditory learners respond well to hearing-oriented phrases like, "How does that sound?" Your kinesthetic learners feel comfortable with phrases like, "How did that exercise feel to you?"

- *Walk around and check on your participants during activities.* Some people finish early and start other conversations; others struggle to get started. Continually move among the groups to keep everyone focused on the task at hand and ensure that they're doing the activity in the way it's intended. Ask questions such as: Did any other questions come up over here? What's the hardest thing about this exercise so far? Is this one working for you? If you see people who remain quiet, try to include them in the discussion with a simple question, or directly ask their opinion.

- *Ask how this information could be applied to the learners' daily activities at various intervals during the session.* This reinforces the concept of taking this learning back into the workplace.

- *Accept that you may not be able to answer all of your learners' questions.* Ask for ideas from the group. Write down the questions you can't answer or have the questioner write it on a sticky note and put it in the "Parking Lot." Then you can get an answer after the class and distribute the answer to everyone by email. The good news is that every question you answer now is a question you'll know the answer to next time around.

- *Anticipate how long each section will take based on the estimates in the sample agendas.* These times give you a general idea of whether you are ahead or behind the schedule so you can make adjustments. If you see that you're falling too far behind, limit the discussion or ask participants to save their questions until the end of the segment. If you're moving too fast, perhaps the participants don't have sufficient time to talk. In that case, stop at the next opportunity and ask for questions on what has been discussed thus far.

- *Make notes of the actual timing of the workshop.* Write the times in the margins of your manual during the class so you can adjust your agenda when planning for future workshop presentations.

If you're running out of time in a class, look through the upcoming exercises and choose those you can cover in discussions instead of using the scheduled exercises.

- ***Read from the resources listed at the end of each module, and study other books that give you additional insight into the topic.*** The more you know, the more confident you'll be in your facilitation.

- ***Create promotional materials using the concepts of advertising and public relations.*** Tie the goals of the courses into organizational goals. Use advertising design and graphics to make communications eye-catching and inviting. Use multiple methods of communication including email, posters, presentations, and one-on-one invitations.

- ***Consider methods to support the transfer of this learning to the workplace.*** Ideas include a follow-up email asking for processes they've implemented as a result of the workshop, or "alumni sessions" to share best practices on the topic.

- ***Finally, be willing to learn along with your participants.*** If you don't know, say so; your homework assignment is to find out. That's the best example any facilitator can set.

In chapter 3, you will learn the concepts that are presented in the customer service skills modules on the basics of customer service, telephone skills, how to deal with difficult customers, and internal customer service.

What to Do Next

When you have determined which workshop you will present, here's what you should do next:

- Study the workshop, read additional materials on the topic, and determine any follow-up activities for the session.

- Set the date, but first check organization calendars, holidays, and other important events that could affect participation.

- Visit the room where you will hold the program to determine the layout of your classroom and how many attendees it will accommodate.

- Create a promotional plan for your workshop, and think of new places and ways to get the word out.

- Review the list at the beginning of your workshop to ensure that you have the materials needed to produce the session.

- Prepare the handouts and purchase all supplies.

- Monitor registration and send confirmation emails.

- Check the room setup and make sure all equipment is working properly.

- Practice the presentation.

- Use meditation, visualization, or any other relaxation technique to focus your energy and mind for your presentation.

Section Two:
Customer Service

Customer Service Skills Overview 3

▲   ▲   ▲

An organization's success in today's marketplace depends on how it attracts customers, retains them, and continually satisfies their needs in a way that develops customer loyalty. The four modules in this section represent the basic skills and competencies needed to develop these elements of customer service excellence.

What's in Each Module?

"Basics of Customer Service" allows employees to step into their customer's shoes and analyze methods to meet and even exceed their customer's expectations. It presents learners with a formula to ensure that they offer customers a consistently high level of service. It also introduces the standards for handling challenging customer situations.

Because a large percentage of business is conducted via the telephone, "Telephone Skills Training" is a session of vital importance. This seminar identifies methods for your workforce to turn every phone interaction into a public relations opportunity through close analysis of phone call greetings and closings, development of formulas for problem solving, and evaluation of the effects of specific word choices and tone. Learners will also practice methods to ensure that their telephone messages achieve the desired outcomes.

The module on "Dealing With Difficult Customers" equips learners with tools and techniques to deal with challenging situations by focusing on the solutions rather than the problems or personalities involved. Sections of this session focus on the skills of active listening, the importance of adopting a customer orientation, and the ability to work in cooperation with others to create solutions for internal or external customer interactions.

Participants who attend the session "Internal Customer Service" will learn to take all the tools of customer service excellence and apply them to relationships within their own workplaces. They'll analyze their internal customer interactions and create systems to improve communications and processes, as well as discover ways to improve their understanding of the various personalities and communication styles of their co-workers. The result will be a better working environment, as well as improved outcomes for external customers.

What Are the Ultimate Outcomes?

These modules create opportunities for the members of an organization to step out of their daily roles and assess interactions from their customer's perspective. As employees stand in the customer's shoes for these four interactive sessions, they will refine their service skills and inspire a sense of loyalty in their customers.

Basics of Customer Service 4

What's in This Chapter?

- Objectives for the half-day customer service workshop
- Lists of materials for facilitator and participants
- Detailed program agenda to be used as a facilitator's guide
- All PowerPoint slides for the workshop

▲   ▲   ▲

"Basics of Customer Service" shows participants how to assess customer expectations and determine how their current activities support those expectations. It encourages learners to change roles, so they view interactions from the customer's perspective. In addition, it gives learners the opportunity to practice their customer service skills in a supportive setting.

The half-day workshop enables attendees to participate in either a discussion or a practice of the skills of each topic of customer service included, and the exercises can be adjusted to allow more in-depth practice, if time is available. At the end of the workshop, learners will commit to action items for continued development.

Training Objectives

The participants' objectives for the half-day customer service workshop are to be able to

- analyze interactions using the customer's perspective
- use the Fantastic Service Equation to create memorable customer experiences
- establish a plan for continued development of customer service skills.

⊙ ✖ Materials

For the facilitator:

- this chapter, for reference and use as a facilitator guide
- Learning Activity 4-1: Introductions
- Learning Activity 4-2: Self-Assessment
  - Assessment 4-1: Self-Assessment
- Learning Activity 4-3: Customer Expectations
  - Training Instrument 4-1: Categories of Customer Expectations
- Learning Activity 4-4: Who Are Your Customers?
  - Training Instrument 4-2: Who Are Your Customers?
- Learning Activity 4-5: Customer Orientation
- Learning Activity 4-6: Fantastic Service Equation
  - Tool 4-1: Fantastic Service Equation
- Learning Activity 4-7: Customer Service Practice
  - Training Instrument 4-3: Customer Service Practice Exercise
  - Training Instrument 4-4: Evaluation Checklist
- Learning Activity 4-8: Putting It All Together
- Assessment 4-2: Program Evaluation
- PowerPoint slide program, titled "Basics of Customer Service" (slides 4-1 through 4-21). To access slides for this program, open the file *UBBS_PowerPointSlides_Ch04.ppt* on the accompanying CD. Thumbnail versions of the slides for this workshop are included at the end of this chapter.
- projector, screen, and computer for displaying PowerPoint slides
- flipchart and markers.

For the participants:

- pens or pencils
- name badges
- set of handouts for each participant
- sticky notepads and markers on each table

- assorted toys and puzzles on each table
- snacks and candy, as desired.

Sample Agenda

Start	Activity	Minutes
:00	Welcome	:05
:05	Objectives and Agenda	:05
:10	Introductions (4-1)	:15
:25	Self-Assessment (4-2)	:20
:45	Customer Expectations (4-3)	:20
1:05	Who Are Your Customers? (4-4)	:15
1:20	Customer Orientation (4-5)	:30
1:50	Break	:15
2:05	Fantastic Service Equation (4-6)	:40
2:45	Customer Service Practice (4-7)	:50
3:35	Putting It All Together (4-8)	:15
3:50	Closing	:10

8:00 a.m.   Welcome (5 minutes)

PPT As participants enter the room, show **slide 4-1** on the screen to greet your learners. Welcome them and introduce yourself. Explain that the purpose of the workshop is to rediscover the basics of customer service by looking at the topic from the customer's perspective.

This discussion can include any specific customer service themes of your organization that the workshop will address. In addition, because the participants are already using many of the practices to be discussed today, this can be a refresher course. The workshop can also remind the participants of some customer service steps that they might have forgotten. Finally, let the participants know that this session is an important opportunity to share the customer service practices that have worked well for them in the past.

Rules

Explain the ground rules for the session. Here are some sample ground rules and housekeeping items:

- Turn cell phones to silent. (Do this to your own cell phone—lead by example and ensure that your phone isn't the one that rings during the session.)

- The handouts are participants' note pages from this session. Learners should follow along and fill in the handouts with information from the workshop discussions so they can refer to them later.

- This workshop is interactive. Participants will benefit most from the ideas and suggestions shared by their fellow learners, so they should be prepared to contribute to the discussions. (You can even use small prizes or other incentives to increase participation in the session.)

- A break is scheduled during the session.

- Restrooms, smoking areas, snacks, and vending machines are located in the following areas: *[add details]*.

- Respectful communication is required. If someone is speaking, please give that person all of your attention.

8:05   Objectives and Agenda (5 minutes)

PPT Present **slide 4-2**, which shows the workshop's objectives. The participants should understand that the purpose of today's session is to remind us of our expectations when we are customers and to enable us to address our customers' needs more effectively.

PPT Show **slide 4-3**, which lists the items on the agenda, and ask participants if they have any questions.

You may also choose to have a copy of the agenda posted in the training room, so learners can refer to it to during the session.

8:10   Introductions (15 minutes)

 Present **slide 4-4** to set the stage for the introductions that will follow. Perform **learning activity 4-1** to help recognize participants' specific needs in the area of customer service.

8:25   Self-Assessment (20 minutes)

 Show **slide 4-5** to introduce the concept of self-assessment. How are the participants doing currently in their customer service skills? Conduct **learning activity 4-2** to allow the participants a chance to assess themselves.

8:45   Customer Expectations (20 minutes)

 Display **slides 4-6 and 4-7** to introduce customer expectations. Note that the areas that the participants found challenging in the self-assessment are not unique. No matter how good our customer service skills are, we can always improve in some areas. Sometimes it just helps to step back and put ourselves in our customers' shoes, so we can remember what's really important to them. The participants will be able to do this as you conduct **learning activity 4-3**.

9:05   Who Are Your Customers? (15 minutes)

Slide 4-8 asks the question, "Who are your customers?" Introduce **learning activity 4-4** by explaining that not every customer is a person who walks into their business or organization to spend money. Tell the participants to take a moment to think about all of the different customers they serve in an average workday.

Ask the participants to consider both internal and external customers as they complete the rest of the activities in today's session.

9:20   Customer Orientation (30 minutes)

Display **slide 4-9** to introduce the topic of customer orientation. Use **learning activity 4-5** and **slides 4-10 through 4-13** to help participants adopt a customer orientation. Tell the participants that after the break they will learn a formula to help them ensure customer satisfaction.

9:50   Break (15 minutes)

10:05   Fantastic Service Equation (40 minutes)

Slides 4-14 and 4-15 highlight the Fantastic Service Equation, which is a formula developed by Maxine Kamin (ASTD, 2002) to help ensure that they meet or exceed those customer expectations every time they interact with a customer. Conduct **learning activity 4-6** so that the participants can familiarize themselves with the Fantastic Service Equation.

10:45   Customer Service Practice (50 minutes)

Show **slides 4-16 and 4-17** to set the stage to use all of the concepts of customer service the participants have learned. Conduct **learning activity 4-7**, in which they will have the opportunity to practice the Fantastic Service Equation and discover how it relates to customer service.

11:35   Putting It All Together (15 minutes)

Show **slide 4-18** to let participants know that it's time to apply the concepts they've learned. Present **slide 4-19** so learners can see the objectives they've met in this workshop. Conduct **learning activity 4-8**. During this activity, the participants will summarize the lessons they learned, answer any additional questions, and create a plan of action for transfer of learning. Remind the participants that a successful learning experience requires time to come up with an action plan, as shown in **slide 4-20**.

11:50   Closing (10 minutes)

PPT Display **slide 4-21** and explain that your contact information is included there. Encourage them to contact you if they have additional questions once they get back into the workplace.

As you close the session, discuss briefly how easy it is to forget about the customer's point of view. Ask the participants what prevents them from being able to practice fantastic service every time, and determine which tools they studied today might help them retain and build on their customer service focus. Remind them that these are the insights you'd like them to keep in mind as they go back to their departments.

 Suggest to the participants that you'd like to continue to develop your skills, too, and that one way they can help you is to fill out an evaluation form. Ask the learners to complete **assessment 4-2** to let you know what they liked or what changes they would like to see. Show them where to leave the forms when they exit the room.

Thank the participants for their attention, and end the session with a motivating story, quote, or anecdote from your personal collection.

 12:00 p.m.   Adjourn

What to Do Next

- Using the material in this chapter as a guide, build a detailed plan to prepare for this workshop.

- To adjust the length of this session, add more discussion time to the Fantastic Service Equation, analyze a participant customer experience using the chain of experience, or add another round of customer service practice. After the initial round is discussed and recommendations are made, participants can make adjustments and see whether they have handled the situations better.

- Schedule a training room and invite your attendees. To build interest, you may change the title of the session to tie in with your industry or business, send an introductory email that includes common customer service concerns in your organization, or include promotional presentations in individual departmental meetings.

- Draft a supply list, teaching notes, and time estimates. To customize teaching notes, print the slides as note pages and add your own notes to ensure that you don't overlook any key points.

- Decide how you will support the learner's action plan. If you want to customize the action plan to your organization, get input from participating department managers on which items they would like to include as action items.

- Consider designing follow-up sessions to encourage the learners to continue to develop customer service skills.

- For additional modules, background information, and extended training sessions on this subject, refer to the resources used in the development of these materials, specifically *Customer Service Training* by Maxine Kamin (ASTD Press, 2002), *Leadership Training* by Lou Russell (ASTD Press, 2003), and *Manager Skills Training* by Christee Gabour Atwood (ASTD Press, 2008).

PowerPoint Slides

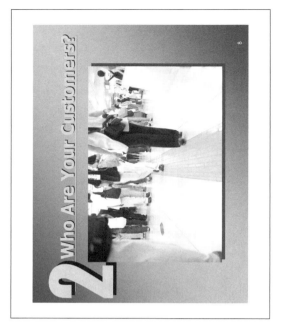

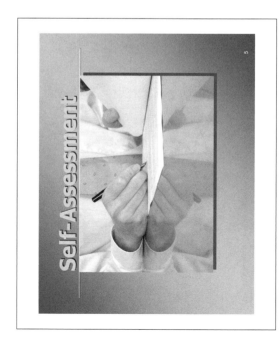

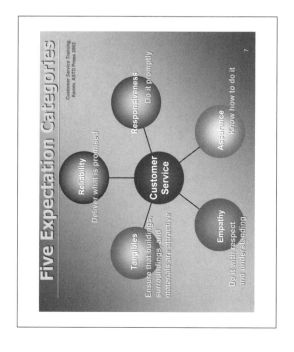

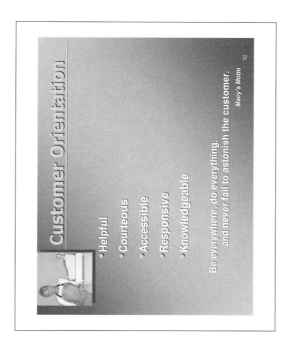

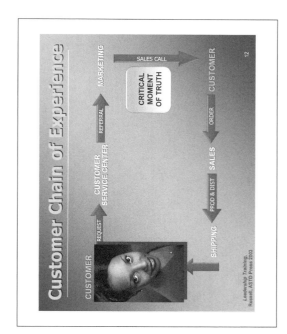

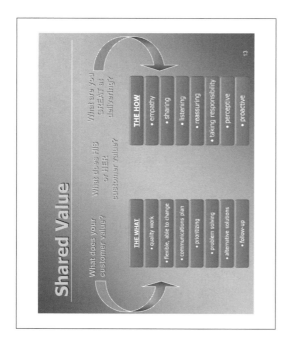

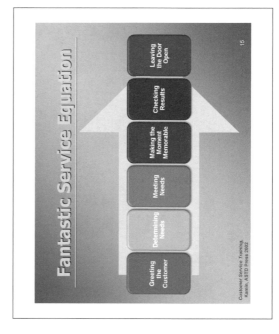

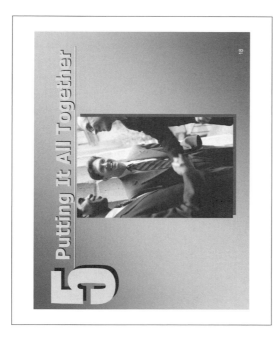

5 Putting It All Together

18

Action Plan

24 Hours:
Ask one customer to rate your service.

7 Days:
Practice the Fantastic Service Equation in a challenging customer situation.

30 Days:
Offer a summary of the Fantastic Service Equation at a staff meeting.

20

Customer Service Practice

• Your group will create a five-minute presentation that shows how you would handle your situation.

• Use the Fantastic Service Equation as a guide and be creative!

• Observers will make notes on their Evaluation Checklists of what they like and any other suggestions they have to handle the situation.

17

Summary

Our objectives today were to learn to

» analyze interactions using the customer's perspective

» use the Fantastic Service Equation to create memorable customer experiences

» establish a plan for continued development of customer service skills.

19

Telephone Skills Training 5

What's in This Chapter?

- Objectives for the half-day telephone skills workshop

- Lists of materials for facilitator and participants

- Detailed program agenda to be used as a facilitator's guide

The telephone skills workshop allows learners to discuss and practice effective ways to present a positive image over the telephone. This information is useful not only for call centers, receptionists, and other personnel who spend large amounts of time on the telephone, but also for any members of the organization who want to update their practices to ensure that they are presenting a quality image for their organization.

The workshop enables attendees to participate in either discussion or practice of the skills in each section by adjusting the time allowed for activities. Please note the changes in time allotment for the learning activities and use the ones listed in the following sample agenda. At the end of the workshop, learners will create an action plan for continued development.

Training Objectives

The participants' objectives for the half-day telephone skills workshop are to be able to

- effectively perform all of the elements of telephone interactions

- use step-by-step procedures to create positive resolutions to telephone challenges

- establish a plan for continued development of telephone skills.

⟳ ✖ Materials

For the facilitator:

- this chapter, for reference and use as a facilitator guide

- Learning Activity 5-1: Introductions

- Learning Activity 5-2: Self-Assessment

  ○ Assessment 5-1: Self-Assessment

- Learning Activity 5-3: What's Wrong With This Call?

  ○ Training Instrument 5-1: What's Wrong With This Call?

- Learning Activity 5-4: Tone of Professionalism

- Learning Activity 5-5: Telephone Body Language

- Learning Activity 5-6: Telephone Professionalism

- Learning Activity 5-7: Telephone Procedures

  ○ Training Instrument 5-2: Telephone Procedures

- Learning Activity 5-8: Telephone Challenges

  ○ Training Instrument 5-3: LAST Formula for Challenging Telephone Conversations

  ○ Training Instrument 5-4: Practice Situations

- Learning Activity 5-9: Putting It All Together

- Assessment 5-2: Program Evaluation

- PowerPoint slide program, titled "Telephone Skills" (slides 5-1 through 5-21). To access slides for this program, open the file *UBBS_PowerPointSlides_Ch05.ppt* on the accompanying CD. Thumbnail versions of the slides for this workshop are included at the end of this chapter.

- projector, screen, and computer for displaying PowerPoint slides

- flipchart and markers.

For the participants:

- pens or pencils for each participant

- name badges for each participant

- set of handouts for each participant

- sticky notes attached to the front of each set of handouts

- assorted toys and puzzles for the participant tables

- snacks and candy, as desired.

🕐 Sample Agenda

START	ACTIVITY	MINUTES
:00	Welcome	:05
:05	Objectives and Agenda	:05
:10	Introductions (5-1)	:15
:25	Self-Assessment (5-2)	:20
:45	What's Wrong With This Call? (5-3)	:35
1:20	Tone of Professionalism (5-4)	:10
1:30	Telephone Body Language (5-5)	:10
1:40	Telephone Professionalism (5-6)	:10
1:50	Break	:15
2:05	Telephone Procedures (5-7)	:40
2:45	Telephone Challenges (5-8)	:50
3:35	Putting It All Together (5-9)	:15
3:50	Closing	:10

🕐 8:00 a.m. Welcome (5 minutes)

`PPT` As participants enter the room, display **slide 5-1**, on the basics of customer service, on the screen. Welcome the participants and introduce yourself. Ask the participants to guess how much of their time is spent on the telephone. Do they ever get off the phone and realize that they didn't accomplish what they had set out to do? Do they find that they are playing phone tag trying to catch up with people? Do they feel as though they could use the telephone more effectively?

Explain that the workshop will develop practices that will help them use their time on the telephone more effectively: to know the purpose of the phone call when they start to talk, and to achieve that purpose by the time they hang up.

You can expand on this discussion to include any specific themes of your organization that are being addressed by the workshop, such as changes to customer service systems, revised focus areas, or increased efficiency.

In addition, this is a good time to mention that they may already be using some of the practices that will be discussed today, so this can be a chance to build upon those practices. Finally, impress upon the participants that this session is an important opportunity to share their expertise of telephone and communication practices that have worked well for them.

Rules

Explain the ground rules for the session. Here are some sample ground rules and housekeeping items:

- Turn cell phones to silent. (Do this to your own cell phone to lead by example and to ensure that your phone isn't the one that rings during the session.)

- This workshop is interactive. The most important things the participants will learn from this class are the ideas and suggestions that are shared by their fellow learners. They should be prepared to contribute to the discussions. (You can even use small prizes or other incentives to increase their participation in the session.)

- A break is scheduled during the session.

- Restrooms, smoking areas, snacks, and vending machines are located in the following areas: *[add details]*.

- Respectful communication is required. If someone is speaking, please give that person all of your attention.

8:05   Objectives and Agenda (5 minutes)

Show **slide 5-2**, which reviews the objectives of the workshop. The participants should understand that the goal of today's session is to make our time on the telephone effective and to represent our organization in a positive light whenever we communicate with others on the phone.

Show **slide 5-3**, which reviews the agenda. Go through each item and ask for any questions.

8:10   Introductions (15 minutes)

Show **slide 5-4**. Explain that you would like everyone to meet each other and that you'd also like them to start to think about telephone practices that they dislike. Conduct **learning activity 5-1**.

8:25   Self-Assessment (20 minutes)

Show **slide 5-5**, which introduces the concept of self-assessment. Conduct **learning activity 5-2** to help the learners assess some specific areas of telephone skills.

8:45   What's Wrong With This Call? (35 minutes)

Show **slide 5-6** as an introduction to customer expectations. Now that the participants have identified the areas they can work on, conduct **learning activity 5-3** while displaying **slides 5-7 and 5-8** to help them consider what happens when telephone interactions are good, as well as what happens when they are challenging. Ask the participants to consider the discoveries from this activity as they go through the different elements of telephone interactions.

9:20   Tone of Professionalism (10 minutes)

Show **slide 5-9**, which focuses on tone, one of the features of telephone presence. Conduct **learning activity 5-4**, which allows learners to understand the importance of tone in telephone conversations.

 9:30   Telephone Body Language (10 minutes)

Show **slide 5-10**, which focuses on body language, another feature of telephone presence. Perform the steps of **learning activity 5-5** to discover the surprising effect that body language has on telephone conversations.

 9:40   Telephone Professionalism (10 minutes)

Show **slide 5-11** to emphasize how important words are to any interaction with the customer. Show **slide 5-12** and conduct **learning activity 5-6**, in which the participants will learn to identify professional language for telephone conversations.

After the break, the participants will practice the telephone customer service steps that can make all the difference in the caller's impression of them and their organization.

 9:50   Break (15 minutes)

 10:05   Telephone Procedures (40 minutes)

Show **slide 5-13**, which is a visual introduction to telephone procedures. Conduct **learning activity 5-7** and use **slide 5-14** to help participants learn about the Fantastic Service Equation and to familiarize themselves with the components of the equation.

Even when people practice all the right procedures, things can go wrong and result in challenging situations. In these cases, the learners should use all the processes discussed in today's session, from tone and professionalism to active listening techniques. When these techniques aren't enough, the learners should address their challenges with the LAST formula, which will be discussed in the next activity.

 10:45   Telephone Challenges (50 minutes)

Show **slide 5-15**, which introduces the important skill of how to resolve challenges. Conduct **learning activity 5-8**. In this activity, which is illustrated by **slides 5-16 and 5-17**, participants will learn how to solve telephone challenges with the LAST formula, an acronym for *L*isten, *A*cknowledge and *A*pologize, *S*olve, and *T*hank.

Next, the participants will have some time to see how they can use this information as soon as they turn their cell phones back on.

11:35   Putting It All Together (15 minutes)

  Show **slide 5-18**, which includes a visual introduction to this section, in which the participants can apply all the knowledge they have learned. In **learning activity 5-9**, participants will create a plan to continue to develop their telephone skills. **Slide 5-19** shows all the objectives the participants have met in this workshop, and **slide 5-20** includes an action plan for one day, one week, and one month after the workshop.

 11:50   Closing (10 minutes)

 Show **slide 5-21**. Note that your contact information is listed on the slide in case the participants think of additional questions once they get back into the workplace.

Close the session by briefly discussing that for most people, a telephone call is the most important way to get an impression of a company. Time spent on the telephone with customers represents some of the most important public relations work we'll ever do. Ask which tools the learners picked up today that might help them to retain and build on their telephone skills. Suggest that these are the insights they should remember as they go back to their departments.

 As you finish, remind the learners that you want to continue to develop your skills too, and that one way they can help you is to fill out an evaluation form so you know what they like or what changes they would like to see. Distribute copies of **assessment 5-2**, and ask the learners to complete it. Point out where they can leave the forms when they exit the room.

Thank the participants for their attention, and end with a motivating story, quote, or anecdote from your personal collection.

12:00 p.m.   Adjourn

What to Do Next

- Using the material in this chapter as a guide, build a detailed plan to prepare for this workshop.

- To adjust the length of this session, add more discussion time to the activity on telephone challenges, or a participant's negative telephone encounter with another organization can be solicited and then analyzed using the elements of a phone call.

- Schedule a training room and invite your attendees. To build interest, options may include changing the title of the session to a catchy tie-in that addresses your industry or business, an introductory email that includes common telephone interactions in your organization, or presentations in individual departmental meetings.

- Draft a supply list, teaching notes, and time estimates. If you'd like to customize your teaching notes, print the slides as note pages and add your own outline to ensure that you don't omit any key points.

- Decide how you will support the action plan to which your learners will commit. If you determine that you want to customize the action plan to your organization, get input from participating department managers on what items they would like to include as action items.

- Consider designing follow-up sessions and activities to encourage the learners to continue to develop telephone skills.

- For additional modules, background information, and extended training sessions on this subject, refer to the resources used in the development of these materials, specifically *Presentation Skills Training* by Christee Gabour Atwood (ASTD Press, 2007).

PowerPoint Slides

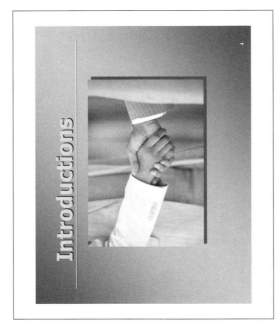

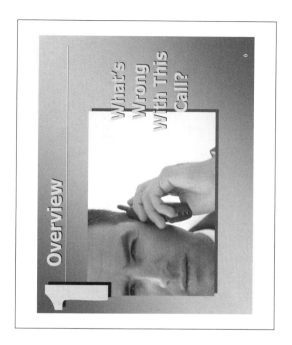

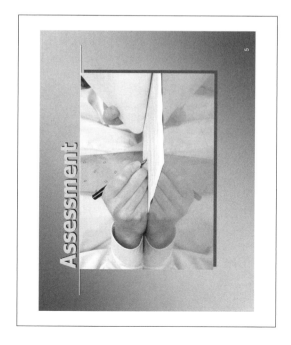

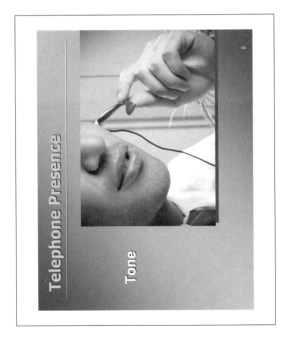

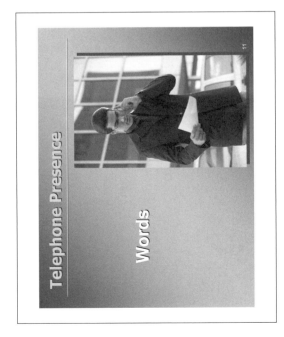

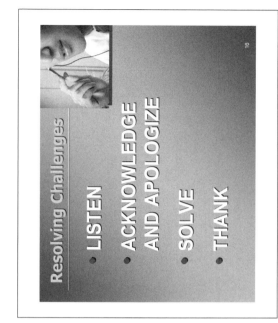

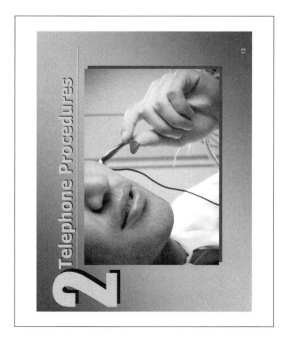

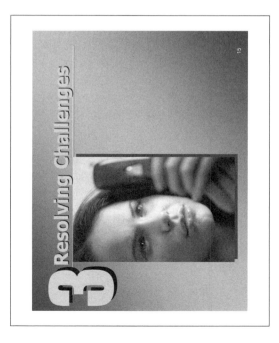

Putting It All Together

5

18

Action Plan

24 Hours:
Create your phone greeting.

7 Days:
Practice the eight great telephone procedures.

30 Days:
Conduct a phone skills survey.

20

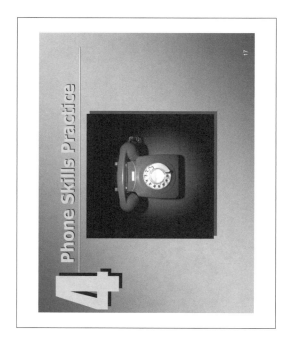

Phone Skills Practice

4

17

Summary

Our objectives today were to learn to

◇ effectively perform telephone interactions

◇ use problem-solving skills for challenging telephone situations

◇ establish a plan for continued development of telephone skills.

19

Dealing With Difficult Customers 6

What's in This Chapter?

- Objectives for the half-day workshop

- Lists of materials for facilitator and participants

- Detailed program agenda to be used as a facilitator's guide

- All learning activities and training documents for the workshop

▲   ▲   ▲

Even those with outstanding customer service skills will encounter challenging situations that require special handling. This session addresses the skills that are of greatest importance during difficult interactions: adopting a customer orientation, using active listening skills, and following a consistent problem-solving formula. The skills practiced in this workshop help learners create positive outcomes from potentially negative situations.

This half-day workshop can be adjusted to allow more in-depth skill practice if time is available. At the end of the workshop, learners will commit to action items for continued development.

Training Objectives

The participants' objectives for the half-day workshop are to be able to

- analyze difficult customer interactions using the customer's perspective

- use problem-solving skills to create positive customer experiences.

◎ ✖ Materials

For the facilitator:

- this chapter, for reference and use as a facilitator guide

- Learning Activity 6-1: Introductions

- Learning Activity 6-2: Self-Assessment

  - Assessment 6-1: Self-Assessment

- Learning Activity 6-3: Customer Orientation

- Learning Activity 6-4: The Difficult Customer

  - Training Instrument 6-1: Techniques for Difficult Customer Situations

  - Training Instrument 6-2: The Difficult Customer Situation

- Learning Activity 6-5: The Angry Customer

  - Training Instrument 6-3: Angry Customer Practice Cards

- Learning Activity 6-6: Problem Solving

  - Training Instrument 6-4: LAST Formula for Difficult Customer Situations

  - Training Instrument 6-5: Problem-Solving Practice Situations

- Learning Activity 6-7: Putting It All Together

- Assessment 6-2: Program Evaluation

- PowerPoint slide program, titled "Dealing With Difficult Customers" (slides 6-1 through 6-21). To access slides for this program, open the file *UBBB_PowerPointSlides_Ch06.ppt* on the accompanying CD. Thumbnail versions of the slides for this workshop are included at the end of this chapter.

- projector, screen, and computer for displaying PowerPoint slides

- flipchart and markers.

For the participants:

- pens or pencils for each participant

- name badges for each participant

- set of handouts for each participant

- sticky notes attached to the front of each set of handouts

- assorted toys and puzzles for the participant tables
- snacks and candy as desired.

🕐 Sample Agenda

START	ACTIVITY	MINUTES
:00	Welcome	:05
:05	Objectives and Agenda	:05
:10	Introductions (6-1)	:15
:25	Self-Assessment (6-2)	:20
:45	Customer Orientation (6-3)	:35
1:20	The Difficult Customer (6-4)	:35
1:55	Break	:15
2:10	The Angry Customer (6-5)	:35
2:45	Problem Solving (6-6)	:50
3:35	Putting It All Together (6-7)	:15
3:50	Closing	:10

🕐 8:00 a.m.   Welcome (5 minutes)

PPT As participants enter the room, have **slide 6-1**, which introduces the concept of dealing with difficult customers, showing on the screen. Welcome them and introduce yourself. Explain that the purpose of the workshop is to help them deal with challenging customers to develop win-win outcomes.

You can expand on this discussion to include any specific customer service themes of your organization that are being addressed by the workshop. In addition, this is a good time to mention that they are already using many of the practices that will be discussed today, so this can be a refresher course for them. The workshop can also remind them of some of the customer service procedures they might have forgotten. Finally, impress upon them that this session is an important opportunity to share their expertise on customer service practices that have worked well for them.

Rules

Explain the ground rules for the session. Here are some sample ground rules and housekeeping items:

- Turn cell phones to silent. (Turn off your own cell phone first, to lead by example and to ensure that your phone isn't the one that rings during the session.)

- This workshop is interactive. The most important things the participants will learn from this class are the ideas and suggestions that are shared by their fellow participants. They should be prepared to contribute to the discussions. (You can even use small prizes or other incentives to increase their participation in the session.)

- The handouts are participants' note pages from this session. They can follow along and fill them in with information from the workshop discussions so they can refer to them later.

- A break is scheduled during the session.

- Restrooms, smoking areas, snacks, and vending machines are located in the following areas: *[add details]*.

- Respectful communication is required. If someone is speaking, please give that person all of your attention.

8:05 Objectives and Agenda (5 minutes)

 Show **slide 6-2**, which includes the objectives for today's workshop. Review the objectives and emphasize that today is an opportunity to stand in the customer's shoes and develop ways to interact more positively, even in difficult situations.

Slide 6-3 lists the five items on the agenda. Go through each item and ask for any questions.

8:10 Introductions (15 minutes)

  Slide 6-4 sets the stage for introductions. Explain that you want everyone to meet each other and that you'd also like to the participants to start to think about those difficult customer situations in which they could use some assistance. Conduct **learning activity 6-1**.

8:25 Self-Assessment (20 minutes)

Show **slide 6-5**, which visually introduces the concept of self-assessment. How are the participants doing right now in their dealings with challenging customer situations? Conduct **learning activity 6-2**, in which the learners will get a chance to assess themselves.

8:45 Customer Orientation (35 minutes)

  Show **slide 6-6**, which introduces the concept of customer orientation. Note that the participant's challenging areas are not unique. No matter how good we are at customer service skills, it is sometimes difficult to see things from the customer's point of view or to stay calm when a customer is agitated. Conduct **learning activity 6-3** and use the debriefing with **slide 6-7** to allow participants to understand their customer's perspective in some of these difficult situations.

Ask the participants to keep the customer's point of view in mind as they work through the rest of the activities.

9:20 The Difficult Customer (35 minutes)

 Show **slide 6-8** to introduce the concept of the difficult customer and then conduct **learning activity 6-4** with **slides 6-9 through 6-12**, which give the learners techniques to handle these situations. As discussed in this activity, customers want to know that people have heard their concerns.

 ### 9:55 Break (15 minutes)

 ### 10:10 The Angry Customer (35 minutes)

 Show **slide 6-13**, which introduces the Angry Customer, and present **learning activity 6-5** with **slide 6-14** to help learners practice their listening skills in angry customer situations. The participants will be able to focus on ensuring the customer's satisfaction, even if a customer has reached the stage of being angry about a situation.

Transition to the next activity by telling participants that there is a formula to help them solve the challenges they can encounter in difficult situations.

 ### 10:45 Problem Solving (50 minutes)

 Show **slide 6-15** to introduce the segment of the program on problem solving. Conduct **learning activity 6-6**, with **slides 6-16 and 6-17** to illustrate the LAST formula for problem solving and to give learners a chance to practice with this formula and to incorporate all of the ideas they've discussed today.

 ### 11:35 Putting It All Together (15 minutes)

 Show **slide 6-18** and note that this is the opportunity to pull together all the concepts that have been discussed today. Conduct **learning activity 6-7** with **slides 6-19 and 6-20** to summarize the objectives learned in this lesson and to present a one-day, one-week, and one-month action plan that the learners can follow to carry these practices back into the workplace.

Congratulate the participants on their active participation in the session.

 ### 11:50 Closing (10 minutes)

Show **slide 6-21** and point out that your contact information is listed on the slide in case the participants think of additional questions once they get back to the workplace.

Close the session by briefly discussing how easy it is to lose sight of the fact that we are all difficult customers from time to time. Ask if the participants had any special realizations today that might help them retain and build on their customer service focus when they deal with difficult customers. Tell them that these are the insights you'd like them to remember as they go back to their workplaces.

Remind the participants that you, too, want to continue to develop your skills and that one way they can help you do this is to fill out an evaluation form to let you know what they liked about the session or what they would like to see changed. Distribute **assessment 6-2**, and have the learners complete it. Point out where they can leave the forms as they exit the room.

Thank the participants for their attention, and end with a motivating story, quote, or anecdote from your personal collection.

12:05 p.m.   Adjourn

What to Do Next

- Using the material in this chapter as a guide, build a detailed plan to prepare for this workshop.

- To adjust the length of this session, you may add more discussion time to the activity regarding difficult customers, analyze a participant's customer experience using the LAST Formula, or add another round of structured experiences after you have discussed the initial round so that participants can make adjustments to improve the way they handle the situations.

- Schedule a training room and invite your attendees. To build interest, options may include changing the title of the session to a catchy tie-in that addresses your industry or business, sending an introductory email about common customer service concerns in your organization, or making presentations in individual departmental meetings.

- Draft a supply list, teaching notes, and time estimates. If you'd like to customize the teaching notes, print the slides as note pages and add your own outline to ensure that you don't omit any key points.

- Decide how you will support the action plan to which your learners will commit. If you determine that you want to customize the action plan on **slide 6-20** to your organization, get input from participating department managers on which items they would like to include as action items.

- Consider designing follow-up sessions to encourage the learners to continue to develop customer service skills.

- For additional modules, background information, and extended training sessions on this subject, refer to the resources used in the development of these materials, specifically *Customer Service Training* by Maxine Kamin (ASTD Press, 2002), *Leadership Training* by Lou Russell (ASTD Press, 2003), *Listening Skills Training* by Lisa J. Downs (ASTD Press, 2008), and *Manager Skills Training* by Christee Gabour Atwood (ASTD Press, 2008).

PowerPoint Slides

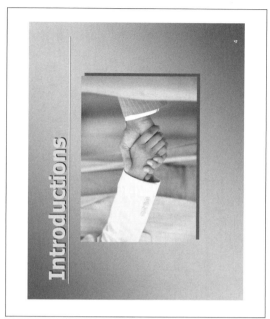

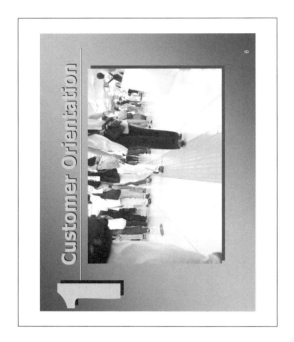

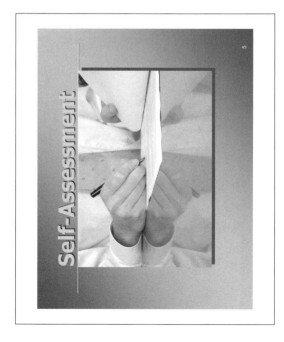

Techniques for
Difficult Customer Situations

☑ Don't blame others.
☑ Avoid 'red flags.'
☑ Don't take it personally.
☑ Take a break.
☑ Use teamwork language.
☑ Get their solutions first.

Difficult Customer Situation

Which techniques
does this
customer service
representative
use?

Techniques for
Difficult Customer Situations

☑ Use active listening techniques.
☑ Allow customers to vent.
☑ Apologize for situation.
☑ Empathize.
☑ Focus on facts.
☑ Lower the volume.

Techniques for
Difficult Customer Situations

☑ Keep a positive tone.
☑ Don't trivialize.
☑ Look for win-win deal.
☑ Use objective party.
☑ End on a positive note.
☑ Any other ideas?

Angry Customer Listening Practice

1. Customer will complain about the situation on the card for 3 minutes.

2. Partner will demonstrate active listening skills.

3. When time is called, partner will summarize.

4. Reverse roles with a new situation card.

14

Apply the LAST Formula

- Listen
- Acknowledge
- Apologize
- Solve
- Thank

16

3 The Angry Customer

13

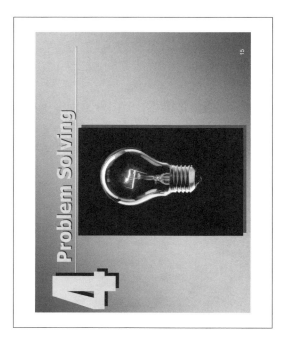

4 Problem Solving

15

Putting It All Together

5

18

Action Plan

24 Hours:
Teach the LAST formula to one person.

7 Days:
Use the LAST formula to solve a customer challenge.

30 Days:
Write an email or memo to your department explaining the LAST formula.

20

Apply the LAST Formula

- Read your customer situation aloud to your group.

- Your group will use the LAST formula to solve this customer challenge.

- Your group will present your solution to the rest of us, using the LAST steps.

- The rest of us will have an opportunity to add suggestions to this solution.

17

Summary

Our objectives today were to be able to

- analyze difficult customer interactions using the customer's perspective

- use problem-solving skills to create positive customer experiences.

19

Internal Customer Service 7

What's in This Chapter?

- Objectives for the half-day internal customer service workshop

- Lists of materials for facilitator and participants

- Detailed program agenda to be used as a facilitator's guide

▲   ▲   ▲

The same skills that can be used to create positive customer service situations with those who use the goods and services of our organizations can be used to create an improved working atmosphere and better outcomes for internal customers. This session takes learners through the processes of applying basic customer service skills, taking time to gain a better understanding of the internal customers with whom they work, and continually surveying co-workers to determine ways to work more effectively with them.

The half-day workshop enables attendees to participate in either discussion or practice of each internal customer service skill included, and the exercises can be adjusted to allow for more in-depth practice, if time is available. At the end of the workshop, learners will commit to action items for continued development.

Training Objectives

The participants' objectives for the half-day internal customer service workshop are to be able to

- assess their current skill level in dealing with internal customers

- adapt their communication styles to achieve improved results

- establish a plan for continued development of internal customer service skills.

⊚ ✖ Materials

For the facilitator:

- this chapter, for reference and use as a facilitator guide

- Learning Activity 7-1: Introductions

- Learning Activity 7-2: Self-Assessment

  ○ Assessment 7-1: Self-Assessment

- Learning Activity 7-3: Who Are Your Internal Customers?

  ○ Training Instrument 7-1: Who Are Your Internal Customers?

- Learning Activity 7-4: Supply and Demand

- Learning Activity 7-5: Intake Styles

  ○ Training Instrument 7-2: Language System Diagnostic Instrument

- Learning Activity 7-6: Recognizing and Overcoming Communication Challenges

  ○ Training Instrument 7-3: Recognizing and Overcoming Communication Challenges

- Learning Activity 7-7: Surveying Your Customers

  ○ Training Instrument 7-4: Internal Customer Service Survey

- Learning Activity 7-8: Putting It All Together

- Assessment 7-2: Program Evaluation

- PowerPoint slide program, titled "Internal Customer Service" (slides 7-1 through 7-18). To access slides for this program, open the file *UBBB_PowerPointSlides_Ch07.ppt* on the accompanying CD. Thumbnail versions of the slides for this workshop are included at the end of this chapter.

- projector, screen, and computer for displaying PowerPoint slides

- flipchart and markers.

For the participants:

- pens or pencils for each participant

- name badges for each participant

- set of handouts for each participant

- sticky notes attached to the front of each set of handouts

- assorted toys and puzzles for the participant tables

- snacks and candy, as desired.

⏰ Sample Agenda

Start	Activity	Minutes
:00	Welcome	:05
:05	Objectives and Agenda	:05
:10	Introductions (7-1)	:15
:25	Self-Assessment (7-2)	:20
:45	Who Are Your Internal Customers? (7-3)	:25
1:10	Supply and Demand (7-4)	:15
1:25	Intake Styles (7-5)	:30
1:55	Break	:15
2:10	Recognizing and Overcoming Communication Challenges (7-6)	:40
2:50	Surveying Your Customers (7-7)	:45
3:35	Putting It All Together (7-8)	:15
3:50	Closing	:10

⏰ 8:00 a.m.   Welcome (5 minutes)

 As participants enter the room, show **slide 7-1,** to introduce the topic of the workshop. Welcome the attendees and introduce yourself. Explain that the purpose of the workshop is to help them discover the positive difference they can make by using the practices of effective internal customer service.

You can expand on this discussion to include any specific themes of your organization that are being addressed by the workshop. In addition, this is a good time to mention that the participants are already using many of the practices that will be discussed today, so this can be a refresher course for them. The workshop can also remind them of some of the communication and service skills they might forget about in the rush of daily activities. Finally, impress on the learners that this session is an important opportunity to share their expertise and practices that have worked well for them in dealing with co-workers and others in the organization.

Rules:

Explain the ground rules for the session. Here are some sample ground rules and housekeeping items:

- Turn cell phones to silent. (Do this to your own cell phone to lead by example and ensure that your phone isn't the one that rings during the session.)

- This workshop is interactive. The most important things participants will learn from this class are the ideas and suggestions that are shared by their fellow learners. They should be prepared to contribute to the discussions. (You can even use small prizes or other incentives to increase their participation in the session.)

- A break is scheduled during the session.

- Restrooms, smoking areas, snacks, and vending machines are located in the following areas: *[add details]*.

- Respectful communication is required. If someone is speaking, please give that person your complete attention.

8:05   Objectives and Agenda (5 minutes)

 Show **slide 7-2** and review the workshop objectives. The participants should understand that the main focus of today's session is to find practices and skills that will help us address our internal customers' needs more effectively and develop a more efficient and harmonious work environment.

 Show **slide 7-3** and go through the five items of the agenda. Ask the participants if they have any questions.

8:10   Introductions (15 minutes)

 Show **slide 7-4,** which sets the stage for introductions. Explain that you want everyone to meet each other and that you'd also like to help them jump-start their thinking about working effectively with everyone else in the organization. Then conduct **learning activity 7-1,** which will help the participants understand the importance of developing relationships with internal customers.

8:25   Self-Assessment (20 minutes)

 Show **slide 7-5** to introduce the concept of assessment, then conduct **learning activity 7-2** (with **Assessment 7-1**), to give participants an idea of the areas they can develop to become stars in internal customer service.

8:45   Who Are Your Internal Customers? (25 minutes)

Show **slide 7-6** to help the participants think about all of the different customers they serve in an average workday. Then conduct **learning activity 7-3** to help them to create their own customer service chain and identify all of their internal customers. Ask the participants to consider all of these customers as they complete the activities in today's session.

Show **slide 7-7,** which reminds the participants that every customer, both internal and external, deserves excellence in service and communication. Although we spend time and effort to ensure that the needs of our external customers are met, we frequently forget that the people we work with, who depend on us to do their jobs, have needs that are equally important.

9:10   Supply and Demand (15 minutes)

 Show **slide 7-8** on supply and demand. Conduct **learning activity** 7-4 to help the participants realize that our relationship with these internal customers influences our workplace atmosphere and also influences the service our organization offers to its external customers.

 9:25   Intake Styles (30 minutes)

 Show **slide 7-9,** on effective communication. Note that internal customers and suppliers create the teams that affect not only the atmosphere of the workplace but also the end product and service that the external customer experiences. Recognizing and respecting the different ways that those customers and suppliers process information can help create more effective communications in their organizations.

  Show the learners' **slide 7-10** as an introduction to communication styles. Now that they've had an opportunity to think about the big picture of internal customer service, ask them to take a step back and look at their own style of communication and interaction with these customers as you conduct **learning activity** 7-5.

 9:55   Break (15 minutes)

10:10   Recognizing and Overcoming Communication Challenges (40 minutes)

Show **slide 7-11,** which lists the features of effective communication. Present **slide 7-12** and then conduct **learning activity** 7-6, which deals with recognizing and overcoming communication challenges. The participants will use the activity to help them discover the types of communications that can help or hinder their success with their internal customers. Note that sometimes, to work more effectively with others, we must adapt how we interact with other people.

10:50   Surveying Your Customers (45 minutes)

Our workplace can be more efficient and pleasant if we take the time to build relationships with our internal customers. We often talk about the Golden Rule and treating our customers the way that we want to be treated. In reality, however, the Platinum Rule is even more effective. It suggests that we should treat our customers in the way *they* want to be treated. The best way to ensure that we offer them the kind of service they want and need is to *ask* them what they want and need.

  Show **slide 7-13** to introduce the concept of building customer relationships. Present **slide 7-14** and then conduct **learning activity** 7-7 to help participants learn to survey their customers.

11:35   Putting It All Together (15 minutes)

  Show **slide 7-15** to remind the participants that now it is time to put together all the things they have learned in the workshop. **Slide 7-16** reviews the objectives that were covered in this workshop and ensures that all of the objectives were met. Conduct **learning activity 7-8** to help the participants create a plan to continue to develop their customer service skills. Remind them that no learning experience is successful unless you take the time to come up with an action plan to put the information to use. **Slide 7-17** gives the participants a one-day, one-week, and one-month action plan.

 11:50   Closing (10 minutes)

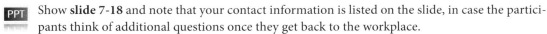 Show **slide 7-18** and note that your contact information is listed on the slide, in case the participants think of additional questions once they get back to the workplace.

Close the session by briefly discussing how easy it is to forget that co-workers are customers too. Ask the learners what sorts of things keep them from being able to practice internal service excellence every time. Which tools did they pick up today that might help them to retain and build on their internal customer service focus? Tell them that these are the insights you'd like them to keep in mind as they go back to their departments.

 Remind the participants that you, too, want to continue to develop your skills, and that they can help by filling out an evaluation form to let you know what they liked or what changes they would like to see. Distribute **assessment 7-2,** so they can evaluate the program. Ask the learners to complete it, and point out where they can leave the forms when they exit the room.

Thank everyone for their attention, and end with a motivating story, quote, or anecdote from your personal collection.

 12:00 p.m.   Adjourn

What to Do Next

- Using the material in this chapter as a guide, build a detailed plan to prepare for this workshop.

- To adjust the length of this session, add more discussion time to the segment on recognizing and overcoming communication challenges, analyze and discuss individual participant's challenges (as long as no names are used), or add more working time to the survey on internal customer service so participants can refine the survey before the end of the session.

- Schedule a training room and invite your attendees. To build interest, options may include changing the title of the session to a catchy tie-in that addresses your industry or business, sending an introductory email that includes common customer service concerns in your organization, or giving presentations in individual departmental meetings.

- Draft a supply list, teaching notes, and time estimates. If you'd like to customize your teaching notes, print the slides as note pages and add your own outline to ensure that you don't omit any key points.

- Decide how you will support the action plan to which your learners will commit. If you determine that you want to customize the action plan on slide 7-17 for your organization, get input from participating department managers on what items they would like to include as action items.

- Consider designing follow-up sessions to encourage the learners to continue to develop customer service skills.

- For additional modules, background information, and extended training sessions on this subject, refer to the resources used in the development of these materials, specifically *Developing Great Managers* by Lisa Haneberg (ASTD Press, 2008), *Customer Service Training* by Maxine Kamin (ASTD Press, 2002), *Teamwork Training* by Sharon Boller (ASTD Press, 2005), and *Leadership Training* by Lou Russell (ASTD Press, 2003).

PowerPoint Slides

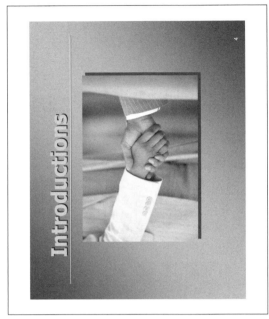

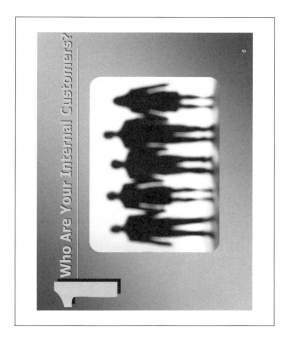

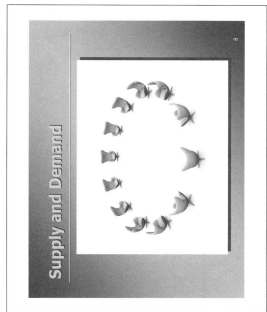

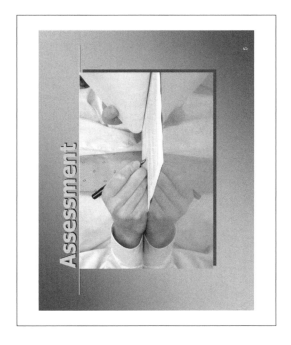

Communication Styles

10

What About YOU?

- How do you enhance or hinder the communication within your team or group?
- What examples are you setting – positive AND negative?

12

3 Effective Communication

Effective communications between internal customers and suppliers create the outcomes that make organizations successful.

9

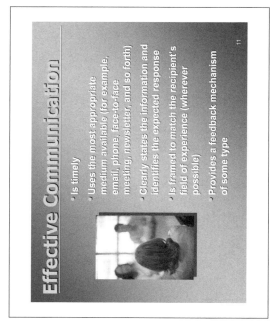

Effective Communication

- Is timely
- Uses the most appropriate medium available (for example, email, phone, face-to-face meeting, newsletter, and so forth)
- Clearly states the information and identifies the expected response
- Is framed to match the recipient's field of experience (wherever possible)
- Provides a feedback mechanism of some type

11

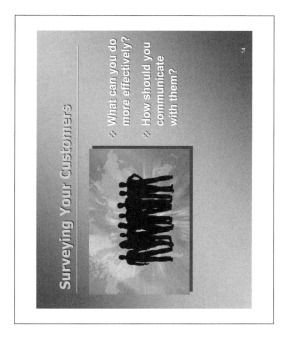

Surveying Your Customers

❖ What can you do more effectively?

❖ How should you communicate with them?

14

Summary

Our objectives today were to learn to

❖ assess your current skill level in dealing with internal customers

❖ adapt your communication style to achieve improved results.

16

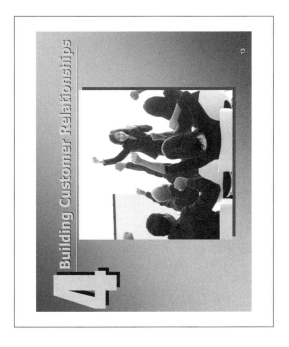

4 Building Customer Relationships

13

5 Putting It All Together

15

Section Three:
Interpersonal Skills

Interpersonal Skills Overview 8

What's in This Section?

- Communication Skills
- Presentation Skills
- Basic Networking
- Conflict Management

▲   ▲   ▲

The four modules in this section represent the interpersonal skills that equip employees to communicate effectively and address the challenges that arise with the diverse thinking of a well-balanced workplace.

Innovative and exciting new ideas must be shared to become reality. Comments and suggestions need to be interpreted in the same positive spirit in which they are given. Effective networking to share best practices creates an even more motivated workforce that is able to apply lessons learned from both inside and outside its four walls.

No one doubts the importance of interpersonal skills, but many think that these skills are inherent and do not need development. True professionals recognize the need for continual development of these abilities and strive to practice their interpersonal skills, improve communication methods, and apply the concepts of emotional intelligence, so they can help create a more cohesive workforce.

What's in Each Module?

In the module "Communication Skills," participants assess their current skill level and determine areas for potential improvement. The session includes a segment on the practices of active listening, which outlines methods to overcome distractions and to interpret spoken and unspoken messages. This program also addresses how to send clear and concise messages, as well as how to align body language and tone with the message being communicated. Other segments include an introduction to the concept of emotional intelligence and an overview of methods to resolve communication challenges.

"Presentation Skills" walks learners through the steps of designing and delivering presentations. The central theme of this workshop is to keep both the goal and the audience in mind when you create presentations. Also included is a segment on the elevator speech, a tool for those who need to learn how to condense messages into the most important points. The module also outlines tips and techniques for proper use of a frequently abused tool, the PowerPoint presentation.

"Basic Networking" guides participants through the necessary steps to develop effective networks so they can create think tanks, conduct benchmarking exercises, and build systems of mentors and collaborators for continual growth. It offers techniques to locate resources to expand networks, as well as ways to build the rapport that creates valuable partnerships.

"Conflict Management" reminds learners that conflict is not necessarily a negative occurrence. It can be negative when it is not addressed correctly, but creatively handled conflict is the basis for taking current processes and advancing them to new levels. This session breaks down the misconceptions about conflict and guides participants through steps to ensure that conflict is applied to build improved systems and stronger relationships.

What Are the Ultimate Outcomes?

When an organization invests time to develop interpersonal skills through this series of workshops, it can help establish more effective communication practices that result in fewer misunderstandings in its workforce. These factors translate to more efficient operations and a higher level of satisfaction for both internal and external customers.

Communication Skills

What's in This Chapter?

- Objectives for the half-day communication skills workshop

- Lists of materials for facilitator and participants

- Detailed program agenda to be used as a facilitator's guide

George Bernard Shaw said, "The single biggest problem in communication is the illusion that it has taken place."

This session permits attendees to practice the essential communication skills needed for success, not only in the workplace, but in all aspects of life. Specific focus is given to active listening skills and the elements of messages that exist beyond the spoken word. The workshop addresses communication challenges through discussion and interactive exercises, and it emphasizes that each individual employee has the power to improve interpersonal interactions in his or her organization.

The half-day workshop enables attendees to participate in either the discussion or the practice of the communication skills included, and the exercises can be adjusted to allow more in-depth practice if time is available. At the end of the workshop, learners will commit to action items for continued development.

Training Objectives

The participants' objectives for the half-day communication skills workshop are to be able to

- demonstrate active listening techniques

- apply the principles of effective interpersonal communications

- establish a plan for continued development of communication skills.

◎ ✖ Materials

For the facilitator:

- this chapter, for reference and use as a facilitator guide
- Learning Activity 9-1: Introductions
- Learning Activity 9-2: Self-Assessment
  - Assessment 9-1: Self-Assessment
- Learning Activity 9-3: The Listening Stick
- Learning Activity 9-4: Effective Listening Behavior
- Learning Activity 9-5: Active Listening Practice
- Learning Activity 9-6: Red Flags
  - Training Instrument 9-1: Red Flags
- Learning Activity 9-7: Body Language
  - Training Instrument 9-2: Body Language
- Learning Activity 9-8: Tone Exercise
  - Training Instrument 9-3: Tone
- Learning Activity 9-9: Interpersonal Skills Practice
  - Training Instrument 9-4: Interpersonal Skills
- Learning Activity 9-10: Putting It All Together
- Assessment 9-2: Program Evaluation
- PowerPoint slide program, titled "Communication Skills" (slides 9-1 through 9-37). To access slides for this program, open the file *UBBB_PowerPointSlides_Ch09.ppt* on the accompanying CD. Thumbnail versions of the slides for this workshop are included at the end of this chapter.
- projector, screen, and computer for displaying slides
- flipchart and markers.

For the participants:

- pens or pencils for each participant
- name badges for each participant
- set of handouts for each participant

- sticky notes attached to the front of each set of handouts

- assorted toys and puzzles for the participant tables

- snacks and candy as desired.

🕐 Sample Agenda

Start	Activity	Minutes
:00	Welcome	:05
:05	Objectives/Agenda	:05
:10	Introductions (9-1)	:15
:25	Self-Assessment (9-2)	:20
:45	The Listening Stick (9-3)	:15
1:00	Effective Listening Behavior (9-4)	:30
1:30	Active Listening Practice (9-5)	:20
1:50	Break	:15
2:05	Red Flags (9-6)	:15
2:20	Body Language (9-7)	:15
2:35	Tone Exercise (9-8)	:20
2:55	Interpersonal Skills Practice (9-9)	:40
3:35	Putting It All Together (9-10)	:15
3:50	Closing	:10

🕐 8:00 a.m. Welcome (5 minutes)

PPT Show **slide 9-1** on the screen as participants enter the room. Welcome them and introduce yourself. Explain that the skills learned in this workshop are completely portable, because no matter where you are—office, social situations, or home—these skills can help you relate better to those around you.

You can expand upon this discussion to include any specific communication themes of your organization that are being addressed by the workshop. Perhaps you would like to develop better interdepartmental collaboration or increased understanding of the chain of processes in your organization. In addition, this is a good time to mention that the participants are already using many of the practices that will be discussed today, so this can be a refresher course for them. Finally, impress upon them that this session is an important opportunity for them to share their expertise and communication practices that have worked well for them.

Rules

Explain the ground rules for the session. Here are some sample ground rules and housekeeping items:

- Turn cell phones to silent. (Do this to your own cell phone to lead by example and to ensure that your phone isn't the one that rings during the session.)

- This workshop is interactive. The most important things the participants will learn from this class are the ideas and suggestions that their fellow learners have shared. They should be prepared to contribute to the discussions. (You can even use small prizes or other incentives to increase their participation in the session.)

- A break is scheduled during the session.

- Restrooms, smoking areas, snacks, and vending machines are located in the following areas: *[add details]*.

- Respectful communication is required. If someone is speaking, please give this person all of your attention.

8:05   Objectives and Agenda (5 minutes)

PPT Show **slide 9-2** and review the workshop objectives on the slide. The participants should understand that the goal of today's session is to practice more effective communication, to help ensure that the message others receive is the same message they intend to send.

PPT Show **slide 9-3**, which lists the agenda items, and ask the participants if they have any questions.

8:10   Introductions (15 minutes)

PPT Show **slide 9-4** as an introduction. Explain that you want everyone to meet each other and that you'd also like them to think about what they'd like to learn from today's workshop. Conduct **learning activity 9-1,** in which participants will discuss the skills of outstanding communicators.

Note that the best way to build on the topics the learners have discussed is to assess where we are right now. That's what this next activity will do for them.

8:25   Self-Assessment (20 minutes)

PPT Show **slide 9-5** to introduce the concept of self-assessment. Conduct **learning activity 9-2 (using assessment 9-1),** to allow participants to assess their areas of strength and potential development in their communication skills.

PPT Next, present **slide 9-6** on effective communications. Now that the participants have determined some areas they'd like to focus on, you can discuss the importance of effective communications and point out the kinds of problems that arise from miscommunication. Ask for examples and include your own stories of misunderstandings and crossed messages.

To continue the discussion, explain that you'd like to begin by studying the most important of all communication skills: the one that's done with our mouths closed.

8:45   The Listening Stick (15 minutes)

Show **slide 9-7** introduce the basics of listening and techniques for better listening. Conduct **learning activity 9-3** to enable participants to experience one level of listening. Ask the participants to build upon the listening skills they've just discussed as you move to the next activities.

9:00   Effective Listening Behavior (30 minutes)

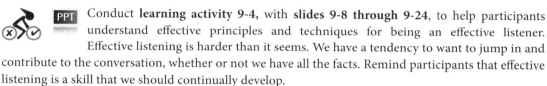

Conduct **learning activity 9-4,** with **slides 9-8 through 9-24,** to help participants understand effective principles and techniques for being an effective listener. Effective listening is harder than it seems. We have a tendency to want to jump in and contribute to the conversation, whether or not we have all the facts. Remind participants that effective listening is a skill that we should continually develop.

9:30   Active Listening Practice (20 minutes)

Conduct **learning activity 9-5** to help learners experience and practice the skill of active listening. This activity illustrates a deeper type of listening than the one the participants experienced in **learning activity 9-3**. When the participants return from the break, they will have an opportunity to study the other side of communications: the messages they send.

9:50   Break (15 minutes)

10:05   The Messages We Send (50 minutes)

Show **slide 9-25,** which introduces the segment on the messages we send. Explain that we send messages every day, and we send many of them without even saying a word. Ask the participants to identify the parts of our messages.

Show **slide 9-26,** which breaks down our messages into three parts: words, body language, and tone. Use the information on the slide to explain the parts of the messages we send. Tell them you'd like to look at each part of those messages individually.

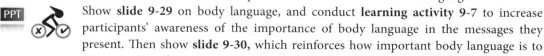

Show **slide 9-27** to introduce the concept of red flag statements. Conduct **learning activity 9-6,** which illustrates how the language used can affect the messages sent. Then show **slide 9-28,** which will help summarize the use of effective language.

Show **slide 9-29** on body language, and conduct **learning activity 9-7** to increase participants' awareness of the importance of body language in the messages they present. Then show **slide 9-30,** which reinforces how important body language is to communication. Summarize effective body language for the learners.

Show **slide 9-31** to introduce the importance of tone of voice in communication. Conduct **learning activity 9-8,** in which participants discover how important their tone is to the messages they present.

10:55   Interpersonal Skills Practice (40 minutes)

 Show **slide 9-32** which introduces interpersonal skills, and then transition into learning activity 9-9 by noting that participants can practice a useful skill that goes beyond simple communication: the ability to interpret what is not being said. Conduct **learning activity 9-9,** using **slide 9-33** as an introduction.

Remind the participants that the most important part of a workshop is to consider how to put all of the new knowledge into action. That's what you'd like them to do now.

11:35   Putting It All Together (15 minutes)

 Show **slide 9-34**, which signals to the participants that it's time to apply the information they have learned. Conduct **learning activity 9-10** with **slides 9-35 and 9-36** to summarize the objectives and help the participants form a plan of action to continue to develop their communication skills after one day, one week, and one month.

11:50   Closing (10 minutes)

 Show **slide 9-37** to conclude the workshop. Point out that your contact information is listed on the slide, in case the participants think of additional questions once they get back to the workplace.

Close the session by briefly discussing how these skills can help create a more effective and pleasant workplace. Many of the challenges that arise between co-workers today come from miscommunications and misunderstandings. Participation in today's session will help remove those miscommunications from the participants' workplaces. Thank the participants for being part of the solution to communication challenges.

 Remind the participants that you also want to continue to develop your skills, and that they can help you by filling out an evaluation form to let you know what they liked about the session or what changes they would like to see. Distribute **assessment 9-2** and ask the learners to complete it. Point out where they can leave the forms when they exit the room.

End the session with a motivating story, quote, or anecdote from your personal collection.

12:00 p.m.   Adjourn

What to Do Next

- Using the material in this chapter as a guide, build a detailed plan to prepare for this workshop.

- To adjust the length of this session, add more discussion time to the section "Putting It All Together" to allow participants to share ideas on specific challenges they are currently experiencing. In addition, add another round of communication challenges after the initial round, so that participants can make adjustments and see if they can improve the way they handle the situations.

- Schedule a training room and invite your attendees. To build interest, options may include changing the title of the session to a catchy tie-in that addresses your industry or business, sending an introductory email that includes the benefits of effective communication in your organization, or doing presentations in individual departmental meetings.

- Draft a supply list, teaching notes, and time estimates. If you'd like to customize your teaching notes, print the slides as note pages and add your own outline to ensure that you don't omit any key points.

- Decide how you will support the action plan to which your learners will commit. If you determine that you want to customize the action plan on **slide 9-36** to your organization, get input from participating department managers on which items they would like to include as action items.

- Consider designing follow-up sessions and emails to encourage the learners to continue to develop their communication skills.

- For additional modules, background information, and extended training sessions on this subject, refer to the resources used in the development of these materials, specifically *Communication Skills Training* by Maureen Orey and Jenni Prisk (ASTD Press, 2004), *Listening Skills Training* by Lisa J. Downs (ASTD Press, 2008), *Teamwork Training* by Sharon Boller (ASTD Press, 2005), and *Promoting Emotional Intelligence in Organizations* by Cary Cherniss and Mitchell Adler (ASTD Press, 2000).

PowerPoint Slides

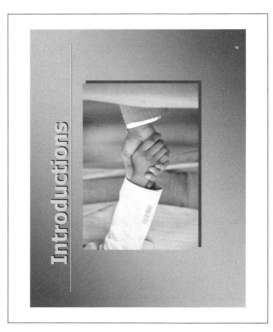

Effective Communications

6

Is Anyone Listening?

- People spend more time each day listening than in any other activity.

- People speak at 100-175 words per minute, but they can listen intelligently at 600-800 words per minute.

What are the implications of this data?

8

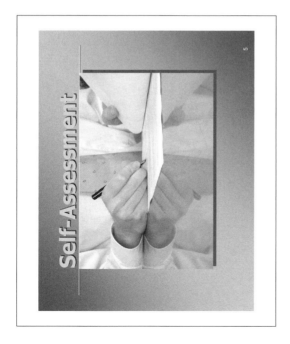

Self-Assessment

5

The Basics of Listening

7

Techniques for Better Listening

- Listeners need to understand their own communication style (strengths and weaknesses).

- Nonverbal communication should be used frequently to provide feedback to the speaker.

10

Techniques for Better Listening

- Go into conversations with an open mind.

- Fully concentrate on the speaker's words and nonverbal cues.

- Separate fact from generalization.

12

Listen Effectively

- Focus on the speaker.
- Ignore distractions.
- Listen without interrupting.
- Acknowledge and confirm understanding.
- Take notes.

9

Techniques for Better Listening

- Be an active listener by listening with a purpose to avoid mind drift.

- Practice listening skills with a trusted friend or family member.

- Provide verbal feedback as appropriate.

11

Techniques for Better Listening

14

- Adopt a caring attitude.
- Determine what information you need to know.
- Be fully present "in the moment."

Informational Listening

16

- **Goal is to receive accurate information from another person.**
- Listening does *not* involve criticizing or judging, only learning.
- Sample scenarios include following directions, exchanging ideas, or learning about someone through personal stories.

Techniques for Better Listening

13

- Keep emotions in check to remain objective.
- Take the orientation of "other" instead of "I."
- Focus only on sound in the foreground.

Four Primary Types

15

- Informational
- Critical
- Appreciative
- Empathic

Empathic Listening

- **Goal is to understand what the speaker is saying and feeling.**
- **It involves making an effort to look at the world through someone else's view.**
- **Sample scenarios include listening to an irate client, helping a friend with an emotional situation, or listening to someone who received bad news.**

22

Techniques for Better Listening

- Adopt a caring attitude.
- Determine what information you need to know.
- Be fully present "in the moment."

24

Tips for Appreciative Listening

- Make an effort to block out background noise.
- Avoid engaging in conversation.
- Turn off electronic devices (such as cell phones, PDAs, and watch alarms).

21

Tips for Empathic Listening

- Paraphrase what the other person says to seek understanding.
- Focus on the speaker's emotions.
- Avoid judging or criticizing; let the person vent if needed.

23

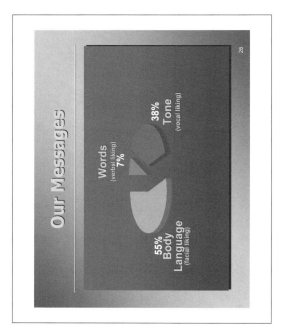

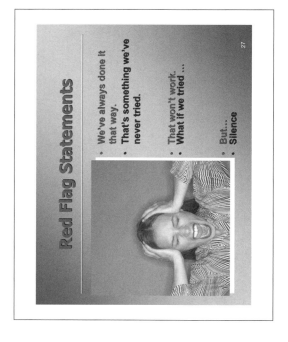

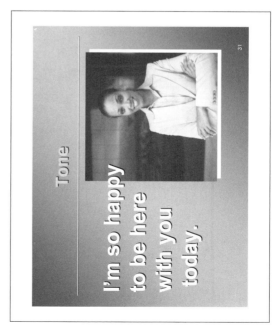

Putting It All Together

5

34

Action Plan

24 Hours:
Teach one concept from today's session to someone.

7 Days:
Practice listening skills in a difficult situation.

30 Days:
Review the Communication Skills Assessment and determine an area for continued development.

36

ACTIVITY

This person has a problem.

You are trying to find out what it is.

33

Summary

Our objectives today were to learn to

- demonstrate active listening techniques

- apply the principles of effective interpersonal communications.

35

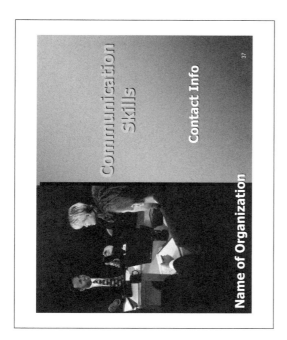

Presentation Skills 10

What's in This Chapter?

- Objectives for the half-day presentation skills workshop

- Lists of materials for facilitator and participants

- Detailed program agenda to be used as a facilitator's guide

The half-day workshop enables attendees to study the process of planning, designing, and writing effective presentations. It also gives participants the opportunity to deliver short presentations to build their confidence level in presenting to groups.

Notes are also included to help the facilitator present this workshop in a longer format by adjusting the exercises and allowing for additional discussion and practice of the techniques presented.

Training Objectives

The participants' objectives for the half-day presentation skills workshop are to be able to

- design presentations that inform, instruct, persuade, or inspire an audience

- practice presentation methods that keep audiences engaged.

⊙ ✖ Materials

For the facilitator:

- this chapter, for reference and use as a facilitator guide
- Learning Activity 10-1: Introductions
- Learning Activity 10-2: Self-Assessment
  - ○ Assessment 10-1: Self-Assessment
- Learning Activity 10-3: Overview
  - ○ Training Instrument 10-1: The SET Formula
- Learning Activity 10-4: Writing Your Presentation
  - ○ Training Instrument 10-2: Presentation Planning Form
- Learning Activity 10-5: Delivering Your Presentation
  - ○ Training Instrument 10-3: Presentation Tips
- Learning Activity 10-6: Group Practice Session
  - ○ Training Instrument 10-4: Guidelines for Visual Aids
- Learning Activity 10-7: Putting It All Together
- Assessment 10-2: Program Evaluation
- PowerPoint slide program, titled "Presentation Skills" (slides 10-1 through 10-20). To access slides for this program, open the file *UBBB_PowerPointSlides_Ch10.ppt* on the accompanying CD. Thumbnail versions of the slides for this workshop are included at the end of this chapter.
- projector, screen, and computer for displaying slides
- flipchart and markers.

For the participants:

- pens or pencils for each participant
- name badges for each participant
- set of handouts for each participant
- sticky notes attached to the front of each set of handouts
- assorted toys and puzzles for the participant tables
- snacks and candy as desired.

⏰ Sample Agenda

START	ACTIVITY	MINUTES
:00	Welcome	:05
:05	Objectives and Agenda	:05
:10	Introductions (10-1)	:15
:25	Self-Assessment (10-2)	:20
:45	Overview (10-3)	:30
1:15	Writing Your Presentation (10-4)	:30
1:45	Break	:15
2:00	Delivering Your Presentation (10-5)	:45
2:45	Group Practice Session (10-6)	:50
3:35	Putting It All Together (10-7)	:15
3:50	Closing	:10

⏰ 8:00 a.m.   Welcome (5 minutes)

PPT   As participants enter the room, display **slide 10-1** as a greeting to your learners. Welcome them and introduce yourself. Explain that the purpose of the workshop is to give them an opportunity to practice their presentation skills in a nonintimidating environment.

You can expand on this discussion to include any specific communication or public relations themes that your organization wants to stress in the workshop. The workshop also reinforces basic communication skills. Finally, impress on the participants that this session is an important opportunity to share questions and concerns as well as share presentation practices that have worked well for them in the past.

Rules

Explain the ground rules for the session. Here are some sample ground rules and housekeeping items:

- Turn cell phones to silent. (Do this with your own cell phone to lead by example and to ensure that your phone isn't the one that rings during the session.)

- This workshop is interactive. The most important things the participants will learn from this class are the ideas and suggestions that are shared by their fellow learners. They should be prepared to contribute to the discussions. (You can even use small prizes or other incentives to increase their participation in the session.)

- A break is scheduled during the session.

- Restrooms, smoking areas, snacks, and vending machines are located in the following areas: *[add details]*.

- Respectful communication is required. If someone is speaking, please give that person your complete attention.

⏰ 8:05   Objectives and Agenda (5 minutes)

PPT Present **slide 10-2,** which reviews the workshop objectives. The participants should understand that the purpose of today's session is to allow us to build upon our presentation skills in a supportive atmosphere.

PPT Show **slide 10-3,** which reveals the agenda for this workshop. Go through each item on the agenda and ask the participants if they have any questions.

⏰ 8:10   Introductions (15 minutes)

  Slide 10-4 sets the stage for introductions. Explain that you want all of the participants to meet each other. One of the best and fastest ways to reduce nervousness is to get to know your audience. In a few minutes, presenting to a room full of strangers can change into talking to a room full of new friends. Next, conduct **learning activity 10-1,** which will help the participants get to know each other.

As you begin **learning activity 10-1**, remind the learners that we all have different levels of comfort with presenting in front of groups. As we've heard so many times, speaking to groups is one of the greatest public fears, so the participants are not alone if they are nervous when they get up to speak.

⏰ 8:25   Self-Assessment (20 minutes)

  Show **slide 10-5** to set the stage for assessment. Conduct **learning activity 10-2** to help the learners assess their level of experience and comfort with public speaking. One way to become more confident in front of a group is to have an understanding of the information you are presenting. In the overview segment that follows, we will explain the formula that will help the learners organize the information in their minds.

⏰ 8:45   Overview (30 minutes)

 Show **slide 10-6** and conduct **learning activity 10-3** with **slides 10-7 through 10-10.** Explain that the SET formula can help the learners create any presentation, whether it's a short impromptu talk or a full presentation.

9:15 **Writing Your Presentation** (30 minutes)

 Display **slide 10-11** to set the stage for this activity. Use **learning activity 10-4** with **slides 10-12 and 10-13** to illustrate the step-by-step method of writing a presentation. Show the learners how the SET (*S*hort answer, *E*vidence, *T*ransition) formula fits into the design of longer talks so they can better organize and write their presentations.

 9:45 **Break** (15 minutes)

 10:00 **Delivering Your Presentation** (45 minutes)

 Present **slide 10-14** to introduce the participants to this activity. Conduct **learning activity 10-5,** which will give ways to make the delivery of their presentations more effective and more comfortable.

 10:45 **Group Practice Session** (50 minutes)

 Show **slide 10-16** to give the participants ideas for the different visual aids they can use to make presentations more interesting. Conduct **learning activity 10-6** to give the learners a chance to use all the techniques they've studied today in a practice session.

11:35 **Putting It All Together** (15 minutes)

Present **slide 10-17.** Conduct **learning activity 10-7** with **slides 10-18 and 10-19** to summarize the objectives that this workshop covered and to present an action plan for the next day, week, and month.

11:50 **Closing** (10 minutes)

Show the learners **slide 10-20** and point out that your contact information is listed on the slide, in case they think of additional questions once they get back to the workplace.

Close the session by reminding them that great ideas can only be enacted if they can communicate those ideas to others. Ask the learners which of the tools they picked up today might help them to retain and build on their presentation skills. Explain that these are the insights you'd like them to keep in mind as they go back to their departments.

Remind the learners that you, too, want to continue to develop your skills, and one way they can help you is to fill out an evaluation form to let you know what they liked about the session or what changes they would like to see. Distribute **assessment 10-2,** ask the learners to complete it, and point out where they can leave the forms when they exit the room.

Be sure to thank them for their attention, and set an example for them with a second closing that ends with a motivating story, quote, or anecdote from your personal collection.

 12:00 p.m.   Adjourn

 What to Do Next

- Using the material in this chapter as a guide, build a detailed plan to prepare for this workshop.

- To adjust the length of this session, add more discussion time to the SET practice, address specific participant concerns and give recommendations, or add another round of presentations with video-taping and evaluations, so participants can make adjustments and see whether they have improved the way they handle situations.

- Schedule a training room and invite your attendees. To build interest, options may include chang-ing the title of the session to a catchy tie-in to your industry or business, sending an introductory email that points out the benefits of presentation skills in your profession, or doing presentations in individual departmental meetings.

- Draft a supply list, teaching notes, and time estimates. If you'd like to customize your teaching notes, print the slides as note pages and add your own outline to ensure that you don't omit any key points.

- Decide how you will support the action plan to which your learners will commit. If you determine that you want to customize the action plan on **slide 10-19** to your organization, get input from par-ticipating department managers on which items they would like to include as action items.

- Consider designing follow-up sessions and activities to encourage the learners to continue to de-velop presentation skills.

- For additional modules, background information, and extended training sessions on this subject, refer to the resources used in the development of these materials, specifically *Presentation Skills Training* by Christee Gabour Atwood (ASTD Press, 2007).

PowerPoint Slides

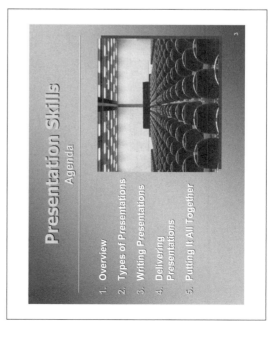

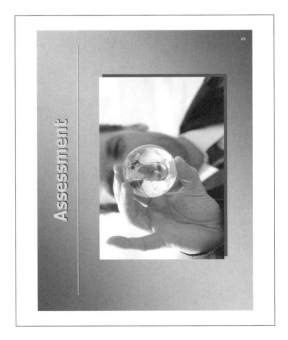

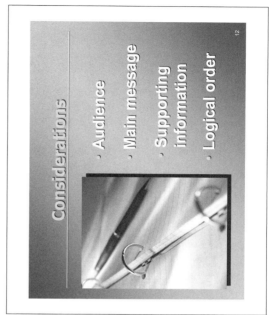

Summary

Our objectives for today's session were to be able to

- design presentations that inform, instruct, persuade, or inspire an audience
- practice presentation delivery methods that keep audiences engaged.

18

Presentation Skills

Contact Info

NAME OF ORGANIZATION

20

4 Putting It All Together

17

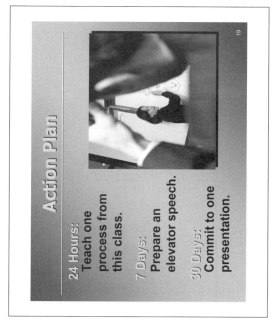

Action Plan

24 Hours:
Teach one process from this class.

7 Days:
Prepare an elevator speech.

30 Days:
Commit to one presentation.

19

Basic Networking 11

What's in This Chapter?

- Objectives for the half-day networking workshop

- Lists of materials for facilitator and participants

- Detailed program agenda to be used as a facilitator's guide

▲   ▲   ▲

Networking is the mechanism that allows individuals to use the power of partnerships and teamwork to develop ideas beyond their own experience, to discover business concepts that could be adapted to their specific needs, to build systems of mentors, and to generate additional business for their organizations. The skills needed for networking include basic communication expertise, the ability to build rapport, and creativity in discovering potential members for networks. These topics are covered in this workshop.

The half-day workshop enables attendees to participate in either discussion or practice of the networking skills discussed in this session, and the exercises can be adjusted to allow more in-depth practice, if time is available. At the end of the workshop, learners will commit to action items for continued development.

Training Objectives

The participants' objectives for the half-day networking workshop are to be able to

- analyze opportunities for increased networking

- use networking skills to develop partnerships and improve working relationships

- establish a plan for continued development of networking skills.

⊙ ✖ Materials

For the facilitator:

- this chapter, for reference and use as a facilitator guide
- Learning Activity 11-1: Introductions
- Learning Activity 11-2: Self-Assessment
  - ○ Assessment 11-1: Self-Assessment
- Learning Activity 11-3: Networking Overview
  - ○ Training Instrument 11-1: Networking Worksheet
- Learning Activity 11-4: Building Rapport
- Learning Activity 11-5: Creating Partnerships
  - ○ Training Instrument 11-2: Planning the Partnership
  - ○ Training Instrument 11-3: Mentoring Considerations
  - ○ Training Instrument 11-4: Mentoring Starter Conversation
  - ○ Training Instrument 11-5: Effective Partnership Self-Check
- Learning Activity 11-6: Putting It All Together
- Assessment 11-2: Program Evaluation
- PowerPoint slide program, titled "Basic Networking" (slides 11-1 through 11-30). To access slides for this program, open the file *UBBB_PowerPointSlides_Ch11.ppt* on the accompanying CD. Thumbnail versions of the slides for this workshop are included at the end of this chapter.
- projector, screen, and computer for displaying slides
- flipchart and markers.

For the participants:

- pens or pencils for each participant
- name badges for each participant
- set of handouts for each participant
- sticky notes attached to the front of each set of handouts
- assorted toys and puzzles for the participant tables
- snacks and candy as desired.

⏰ Sample Agenda

START	ACTIVITY	MINUTES
:00	Welcome	:05
:05	Objectives and Agenda	:05
:10	Introductions (11-1)	:15
:25	Self-Assessment (11-2)	:20
:45	Networking Overview (11-3)	:60
1:45	Break	:15
2:00	Building Rapport (11-4)	:60
3:00	Creating Partnerships (11-5)	:35
3:35	Putting It All Together (11-6)	:15
3:50	Closing	:10

⏰ 8:00 a.m. Welcome (5 minutes)

 As participants enter the room, display **slide 11-1** as a greeting to your learners. Welcome them and introduce yourself. Explain that the purpose of the workshop is to discover the art of networking and the difference it can make to their careers.

You can expand on this discussion to include any specific partnerships in which your organization is currently involved and how those have benefited business. In addition, this is a good time to mention that the participants are already using some of the practices that will be discussed today, so this session will give them ideas to build on those practices even more. Finally, impress upon the learners that this session is an important opportunity to share the networking practices that have worked well for them.

Rules

Explain the ground rules for the session. Here are some sample ground rules and housekeeping items:

- Turn cell phones to silent. (Do this to your own cell phone to lead by example and ensure that your phone isn't the one that rings during the session.)

- This workshop is interactive. The most important things the participants will learn from this class are the ideas and suggestions shared by their fellow learners. They should be prepared to contribute to the discussions. (You can even use small prizes or other incentives to increase their participation in the session.)

- A break is scheduled during the session.

- Restrooms, smoking areas, snacks, and vending machines are located in the following areas: *[add details].*

- Respectful communication is required. If someone is speaking, please give your full attention to that person.

⏰ 8:05 Objectives and Agenda (5 minutes)

 Show **slide 11-2** to review the workshop objectives. The learners should understand that today's session is designed to help them build partnerships that will make them more effective in their current roles and even help them as they move into more advanced roles in the organization.

Present the agenda items on **slide 11-3,** and ask the learners for any questions.

⏰ 8:10 Introductions (15 minutes)

 Use the visual aid in **slide 11-4** to emphasize that you want everyone to meet each other. Explain that you'd also like to start to get a basis for their discussions today on the value of networking. Conduct **learning activity 11-1** to help them meet others in the room and to have an opportunity to practice their networking skills.

Now that they have met the other learners in the room, it's time to see how they could make those introductions even more effective.

⏰ 8:25 Self-Assessment (20 minutes)

 Show **slide 11-5** to introduce the concept of assessment. Conduct **learning activity 11-2,** which will help them assess their strengths and weaknesses in networking. Once they've identified some areas of networking that they can develop, it's time for a basic overview of the range of activities included under the umbrella term *networking*.

⏰ 8:45 Networking Overview (60 minutes)

Present **slide 11-6,** so learners can think about the value of networking in their lives. Use **learning activity 11-3** and **slides 11-7 through 11-22** to present the key principles of networking.

Conclude this section with a discussion of some of the many online networking opportunities available, as well as their benefits. If possible, provide a computer with Internet access, so participants can look at one of the business networking sites (such as LinkedIn) during the break.

Remind the learners that the best networking tools and activities will not be effective without the ability to connect with those individuals and build rapport. That will be the focus when they return from the break.

⏰ 9:45 Break (15 minutes)

10:00   Building Rapport (60 minutes)

 Show **slide 11-23** as a visual aid to introduce the concept of building rapport. Use **learning activity 11-4** and **slide 11-24** to suggest to the learners ways to build rapport and relationships. The next activity will take networking to the next level by helping to develop partnerships.

 11:00   Creating Partnerships (35 minutes)

 Show **slide 11-25** to introduce the section on developing partnerships. Conduct **learning activity 11-5** while showing **slides 11-25 and 11-26.** This will help the participants learn to create mutually beneficial partnerships. Remind participants that the saying "Together everyone achieves more" is true not only within established teams, but also in considering the creation of networks across professions and interest groups.

Remind the participants that no learning experience is successful unless you take the time to come up with immediate steps to reinforce the information in your mind.

 11:35   Putting It All Together (15 minutes)

Show **slide 11-27** to begin the summary of the program. Conduct **learning activity 11-6** with **slides 11-28 and 11-29** to remind the participants of the objectives they have met in this workshop, and encourage them to follow the action plan one day, one week, and one month after the presentation.

11:45   Closing (10 minutes)

Display **slide 11-30** and remind the participants that your contact information is listed on the slide, in case they have additional questions when they get back to the workplace.

Close the session by briefly discussing with the participants how valuable networks can be to them. Ask them how they're planning to use the networks they will develop. Suggest that they think about how the tools they learned today might help them to retain and build on their networking efforts. Tell the learners that these are the insights they should remember as they go back to their departments.

Remind them that you, too, want to continue to develop your skills, and that they can help you by filling out an evaluation form to let you know what they liked or what changes they would like to see. Distribute **assessment 11-2,** ask the learners to complete it, and point out where they can leave the forms when they exit the room.

Thank the learners for their attention, and end with a motivating story, quote, or anecdote from your personal collection.

12:00 p.m.   Adjourn

What to Do Next

- Using the material in this chapter as a guide, build a detailed plan to prepare for this workshop.

- To adjust the length of this session, add more discussion time to the section on network development, analyze a specific networking experience, or add another round to the activity on building rapport.

- Schedule a training room and invite your attendees. To build interest, options may include changing the title of the session to a catchy tie-in that addresses your industry or business, sending an introductory email that includes some of the benefits of networking in your industry, or doing presentations in individual departmental meetings.

- Draft a supply list, teaching notes, and time estimates. If you'd like to customize your teaching notes, print the slides as note pages and add your own outline to ensure that you don't omit any key points.

- Decide how you will support the action plan to which your learners will commit. If you determine that you want to customize the action plan on **slide 11-29** to your organization, get input from participating department managers on which items they would like to include as action items.

- Consider designing follow-up sessions or emails to encourage the learners to continue to develop networking skills.

- For additional modules, background information, and extended training sessions on this subject, refer to the resources used in the development of these materials, specifically *Infoline* No. 250504 "Performance Excellence Through Partnering," *Infoline* No. 250004 "Mentoring," and *Sales Training* by Jim Mikula (ASTD Press, 2003),

PowerPoint Slides

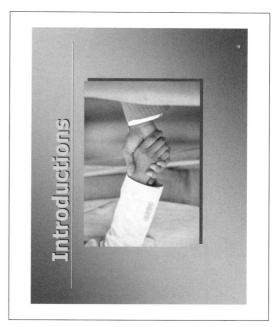

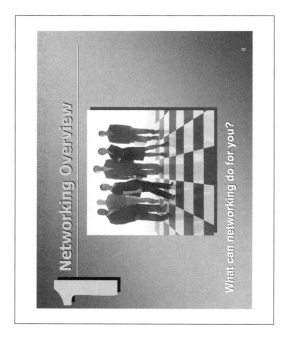

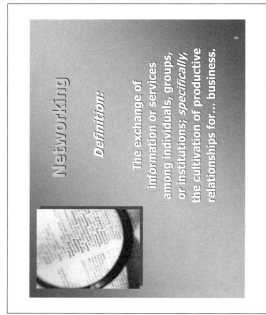

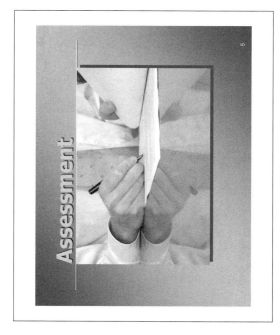

Networking

What
networks
do you
already
participate
in?

10

Networking

Give

- Outflow value to individuals and the network.
- Focus on giving more than you ever hope to receive.
- Separate giving from receiving.

12

Networking

Six Degrees of Separation

- 1960s psychologist Stanley Milgram conducted an experiment.
  - People in Omaha, Nebraska, were sent 160 packets.
  - They instructed recipients to mail the packet to a friend or acquaintance who would be likely to get it closer to the intended recipient in Boston.
- Most of the packets reached the final destination in five or six steps.
  - All of this occurred before faxes or email existed!

9

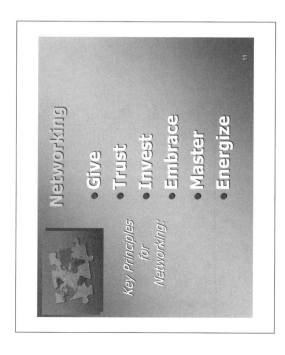

Networking

Key Principles for Networking:

- **Give**
- **Trust**
- **Invest**
- **Embrace**
- **Master**
- **Energize**

11

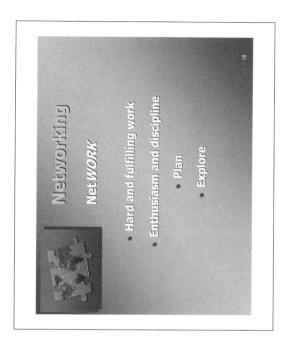

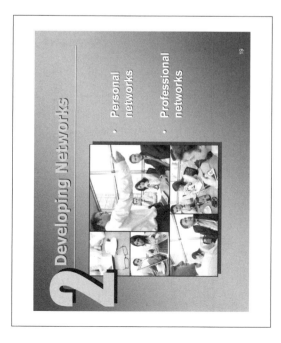

Slide 18 — Networking

*Net**WORK***

- Hard and fulfilling work
- Enthusiasm and discipline
  - Plan
  - Explore

Slide 20 — Practice

- Write one idea on a page about one of the different networks that are available.
- Your facilitator will place the notes on the wall.
- As a class, review all of the ideas and select the top 10.

Slide 17 — Networking

Energize

- The more energy you send out, the more people will be attracted to you.

Slide 19 — Developing Networks

- Personal networks
- Professional networks

2

Recap

- What have you learned from this information?
- What will you use right away in your work? Why?
- How will you use what you have learned?
- What is an effective way for you to actively improve your networking skills? Why?
- How will you know that your actions produce results?

22

Building Rapport

- Find common factors.
- Listen more than you talk.
- Practice active listening skills.
- Be yourself.

24

Practice

- From the top 10 ideas, select which networks you would like to join.
- With a partner and using the Networking Worksheet, develop
  - networking strategies
  - tactics . . . first steps
  - measurements of success.
    - Share your worksheets with the class.

21

Building Rapport

3

23

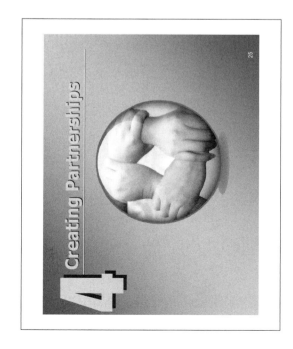

Conflict Management 12

What's in This Chapter?

- Objectives for the half-day conflict management workshop
- Lists of materials for facilitator and participants
- Detailed program agenda to be used as a facilitator's guide

▲   ▲   ▲

This workshop addresses conflict as an opportunity for improving processes, opening up communication channels, and building stronger relationships. Learners will have an opportunity to assess their abilities, identify areas for improvement in their conflict management skills, and practice conflict resolution techniques during the course of this workshop.

The half-day workshop enables attendees to participate in either discussion or practice of the conflict management skills included, and the exercises can be adjusted to allow more in-depth practice, if time is available. At the end of the workshop, learners will commit to action items for continued development.

Training Objectives

The participants' objectives for the half-day workshop are to be able to

- analyze conflicts and determine step-by-step actions to resolve them
- use effective communication styles to discover underlying issues and potential solutions
- establish a plan for continued development of conflict management skills.

◉ ✖ Materials

For the facilitator:

- this chapter, for reference and use as a facilitator guide
- Learning Activity 12-1: Introductions
- Learning Activity 12-2: Self-Assessment
  ○ Assessment 12-1: Self-Assessment
- Learning Activity 12-3: An Overview of Conflict
- Learning Activity 12-4: 10 Questions About Conflict
- Learning Activity 12-5: Personalities in Conflict
  ○ Training Instrument 12-1: Quick n' Dirty DISC Assessment
- Learning Activity 12-6: Resolving Conflict
  ○ Training Instrument 12-2: Resolving Conflict
  ○ Training Instrument 12-3: Conflict Management Strategies
- Learning Activity 12-7: Figuring Things Out
  ○ Training Instrument 12-4: Figuring Things Out
- Learning Activity 12-8: Putting It All Together
- Assessment 12-2: Program Evaluation
- PowerPoint slide program, titled "Conflict Management" (slides 12-1 through 12-34). To access slides for this program, open the file *UBBB_PowerPointSlides_Ch12.ppt* on the accompanying CD. Thumbnail versions of the slides for this workshop are included at the end of this chapter.
- projector, screen, and computer for displaying slides
- flipchart and markers.

For the participants:

- pens or pencils for each participant
- name badges for each participant
- set of handouts for each participant
- sticky notes attached to the front of each set of handouts
- assorted toys and puzzles for the participant tables
- snacks and candy as desired.

⏰ Sample Agenda

Start	Activity	Minutes
:00	Welcome	:05
:05	Objectives/Agenda	:05
:10	Introductions (12-1)	:15
:25	Self-Assessment (12-2)	:20
:45	An Overview of Conflict (12-3)	:35
1:20	10 Questions About Conflict (12-4)	:30
1:50	Break	:15
2:05	Personalities in Conflict (12-5)	:30
2:35	Conflict Resolution (12-6)	:35
3:10	Figuring Things Out (12-7)	:25
3:35	Putting It All Together (12-8)	:15
3:50	Closing	:10

⏰ 8:00 a.m.   Welcome (5 minutes)

PPT   As participants enter the room, display **slide 12-1** as a greeting to your learners. Welcome them and introduce yourself. Explain that the purpose of the workshop is to discover the opportunities and good points about conflict, as well as how to address situations in which viewpoints conflict with each other.

You can expand on this discussion to include any specific themes of your organization being addressed by the workshop, such as new technology or process changes. In addition, this is a good time to mention that the participants are probably using some of the practices that will be discussed today, so this workshop can serve as a refresher for them. The session also can remind them of some of the steps of conflict management that they might have forgotten. Finally, impress upon the participants that this session is an important opportunity to share their expertise and practices that have worked well for them in the past.

Rules

Explain the ground rules for the session. Here are some sample ground rules and housekeeping items:

- Turn cell phones to silent. (Turn your own cell phone off to lead by example and ensure that your phone isn't the one that rings during the session.)

- This workshop is interactive. The most important things participants will learn from this class are the ideas and suggestions shared by their fellow learners. They should be prepared to contribute to the discussion. (You can even use small prizes or other incentives to increase their participation in the session.)

- A break is scheduled during the session.

- Restrooms, smoking areas, snacks, and vending machines are located in the following areas: *[add details]*.

- Respectful communication is required. If someone is speaking, please give that person your complete attention.

⏰ 8:05 Objectives and Agenda (5 minutes)

PPT Review the workshop objectives on **slide 12-2.** The learners should understand that today's session will show us that not all conflict is a negative experience, and that diverse viewpoints are all valuable in reaching resolution in a conflict situation.

PPT Go through the agenda items on **slide 12-3,** and ask the participants for any questions.

⏰ 8:10 Introductions (15 minutes)

PPT Show **slide 12-4** as a visual aid to emphasize that you want everyone to meet each other. Explain that you'd also like to get an idea of the areas of conflict management that they'd like to study today.

Conduct **learning activity 12-1,** which will help the learners meet people and become comfortable in the learning environment. The activity will also allow them to share concerns about conflict management with the other participants. Reassure them that their concerns are not unique and that you'll try to get their questions answered during the course of today's session.

⏰ 8:25 Self-Assessment (20 minutes)

PPT Display **slide 12-5** as an introduction to the concept of assessment. Use **learning activity 12-2** to help the participants assess their areas of strength and weakness in conflict management. Once they've chosen specific areas on which they can focus today, you'll present some of the basics the learners need to understand about managing conflict.

⏰ 8:45 An Overview of Conflict (35 minutes)

PPT Show **slide 12-6,** which begins the overview of conflict, and conduct **learning activity 12-3** with **slides 12-7 and 12-8** to identify the methods that individuals often use to address conflict. Explain that one of the ways we remove some of the negativity about conflict is to do our homework before we address conflict situations. The next exercise will help them do just that.

⏰ 9:20 10 Questions About Conflict (30 minutes)

PPT Show **slide 12-9.** Conduct **learning activity 12-4** to help the learners to understand conflict before they address conflict situations.

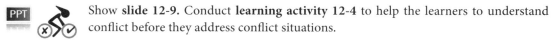

🕐 **9:50   Break** (15 minutes)

🕐 **10:05   Personalities in Conflict** (30 minutes)

Show **slide 12-10** to introduce the learners to the topic of personalities in conflict. Use **learning activity 12-5** and **slides 12-11 through 12-20** to help the participants learn about different personality types and how to adapt communication styles to address them. This can help with the collaboration needed to create resolutions to conflict.

🕐 **10:35   Conflict Resolution** (35 minutes)

This segment will discuss strategies and steps for conflict resolution. **Slide 12-21** introduces the learner to the concept of resolving conflict. Use **learning activity 12-6** with **slides 12-22 through 12-24** to practice the skills of conflict resolution by addressing a specific situation and proposing solutions.

🕐 **11:10   Figuring Things Out** (25 minutes)

Show **slide 12-25**, then conduct **learning activity 12-7** with **slides 12-26 through 12-30** to practice conflict resolution as you consider different cultures and values that can play a part in these difficult situations. Remind the participants that no learning experience is successful unless you take the time to come up with an action plan to put the information to use.

🕐 **11:35   Putting It All Together** (15 minutes)

Show **slide 12-31** to indicate to the learners that it's time to apply the things they've gleaned from this workshop. Use **learning activity 12-8** and **slides 12-32 and 12-33** to review objectives and create a plan for continuing to develop the participants' conflict management skills.

🕐 **11:50   Closing** (10 minutes)

Display **slide 12-34** to conclude the workshop. Remind the participants that your contact information is listed on the slide, in case they think of additional questions once they get back to the workplace.

Close the session by briefly discussing how easy it is to get caught up in conflict and lose perspective. Ask the learners which of the tools they picked up today might help them to stay objective and handle conflict situations more effectively. Tell them that these are the insights you'd like them to remember as they go back to their departments.

Remind the learners that you, too, want to continue to develop your skills, and that they can help by filling out an evaluation form to let you know what they liked or what changes they would like to see. Distribute **assessment 12-2**, and ask the learners complete it. Point out where they can leave the forms when they exit the room.

Thank the participants for their attention, and end with a motivating story, quote, or anecdote from your personal collection.

 12:00 p.m.   Adjourn

 ## What to Do Next

- Using the material in this chapter as a guide, build a detailed plan to prepare for this workshop.

- To adjust the length of this session, add more discussion time to the segment on conflict resolution practice, analyze a participant's conflict management experience using the tools of the session, or add another round of resolving conflict practice after the initial round is discussed and recommendations are made, so that participants can make adjustments and see if they have improved the way they handle the situations.

- Schedule a training room and invite your attendees. To build interest, options may include changing the title of the session to a catchy tie-in to your industry or business, sending an introductory email that includes common causes of conflict in your organization, or doing presentations in individual departmental meetings.

- Draft a supply list, teaching notes, and time estimates. If you'd like to customize your teaching notes, you can print the slides as note pages and add your own outline to ensure that you don't omit any key points.

- Decide how you will support the action plan to which your learners will commit. If you determine that you want to customize the action plan on slide 12-33 to your organization, get input from participating department managers on what items they would like to include as action items.

- Consider designing follow-up sessions to encourage the learners to continue to develop conflict management skills.

- For additional modules, background information, and extended training sessions on this subject, refer to the resources used in the development of these materials, specifically *Diversity Training* by Cris Wildermuth and Susan Gray (ASTD Press, 2005), *Communication Skills Training* by Maureen Orey and Jenni Prisk (ASTD Press, 2004), *Leadership Training* by Lou Russell (ASTD Press, 2003), *Manager Skills Training* by Christee Gabour Atwood (ASTD Press, 2008) and *Put Emotional Intelligence to Work* by Jeff Feldman and Karl Mulle (ASTD Press, 2007).

PowerPoint Slides

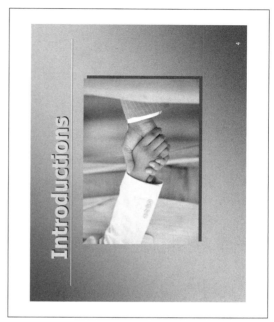

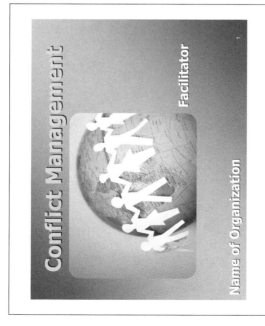

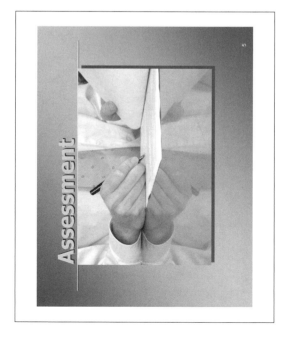

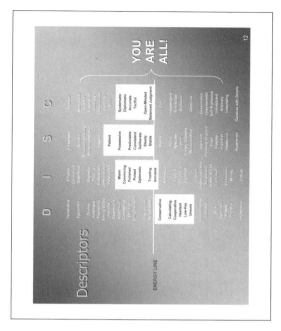

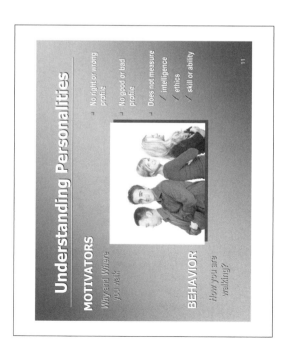

Dominance

Characteristics
- Direct
- Decisive
- High ego strength
- Problem solver
- Risk taker
- Blunt
- Results-oriented

Communication Tips
- Be brief and direct.
- Don't ramble.
- Bring suggestions.
- Focus on business.
- Support statements with facts.

14

Steadiness

Characteristics
- Good listener
- Steady
- Peacemaker
- Predictable
- Understanding
- Possessive
- Friendly

Communication Tips
- Create a favorable environment.
- Express interest in him or her as a person.
- Don't be aggressive.
- Give them time to adjust to changes.
- Define how this fits into the big picture.

16

Best Methods of Communicating

- Which personality are you?
- How should we communicate with you?

13

Influence

Characteristics
- Enthusiastic
- Trusting
- Persuasive
- Talkative
- Impulsive
- Emotional
- Optimistic

Communication Tips
- Create a friendly environment.
- Allow them to vent.
- Allow time for sociable activities.
- Submit details in writing.
- Develop a participative relationship.

15

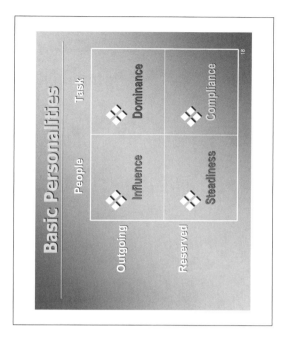

Basic Personalities

	People	Task
Outgoing	Influence	Dominance
Reserved	Steadiness	Compliance

18

Reacting to Difficult Personalities

- Unresponsive: Ask open-ended questions. Be silent and wait for responses. Be patient and positive.

- Egoist: Make sure you know the facts. Agree when possible. Ask questions and listen. Disagree only when you *know you are right.*

20

Compliance

Characteristics	Communication Tips
· Accurate	· Be organized.
· Conscientious	· Prepare pros and cons of proposed ideas.
· Careful	· Support ideas with data.
· Precise	· No surprises!
· High standards	· Disagree with facts, not with the person.
· Systematic	· Be patient and diplomatic.
· Fact-finder	

17

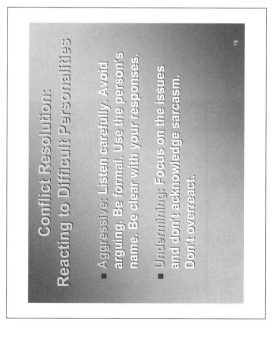

Conflict Resolution:
Reacting to Difficult Personalities

- Aggressive: Listen carefully. Avoid arguing. Be formal. Use the person's name. Be clear with your responses.

- Undermining: Focus on the issues and don't acknowledge sarcasm. Don't overreact.

19

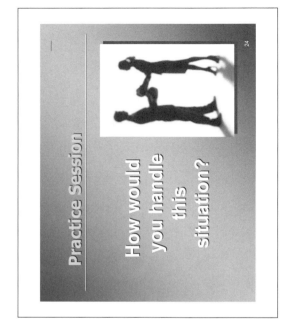

Personal Commitment

- How can you apply what you learned?
- What one thing do you plan to do as a result of today's discussions?

30

Summary

Our objectives today were to learn to

- ❖ analyze conflict situations to determine potential resolutions

- ❖ use effective communication styles for various personalities involved in conflict situations.

32

Figuring Things Out

- What could be the payoff?
- Can you think of situations in which this would be a useful tool?
- How can you use conversity (discussion to discover connections and similarities) to conciliate differences in values?

29

Putting It All Together

4

31

Action Plan

24 Hours:
Observe those around you to determine personality types.

7 Days:
Use the strategies of conflict management to solve a problem.

30 Days:
Talk to those you work with about the best methods to communicate with them.

33

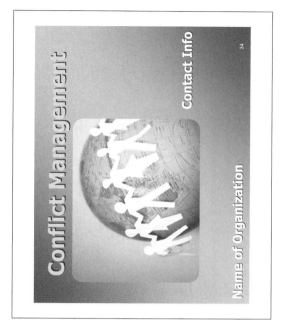

Conflict Management

Contact Info

Name of Organization

34

Section Four:
Basic Business Skills

Business Skills Overview   13

What's in This Section?

- Priority Management

- Decision Making and Problem Solving

- Business Writing and Email

- Basic Business Knowledge

The four modules in this section represent the basic business skills that create efficiency and productivity in daily processes. This knowledge produces improved outcomes for the organization and results in well-rounded employees who represent the organization in a positive light through their actions and the communications that they produce.

Employees are motivated when they know where their positions fit into the framework of the organization; it helps them understand the processes and why the daily activities that might otherwise seem less critical are actually part of a much bigger picture.

What's in Each Module?

The module "Priority Management" introduces participants to methods that organize the overload of information that they face each day. A segment on time management helps them assign priorities and create action plans for their activities. Project management techniques allow them to take their own personal time management procedures and adapt them to situations where they are working on larger projects, whether alone or as part of a team. Records management guides them through systems so they can catalogue and retrieve the information they need. The program also includes a segment on how to manage those real-world challenges and time wasters that can make it more difficult to accomplish their tasks.

The module "Decision Making and Problem Solving" establishes a standardized process for participants to ensure that they take all factors into account when they make decisions. They will learn to weigh the benefits of each solution and determine which is most suited to obtaining the outcome they require. The program also allows learners to practice problem solving in teams that include diverse viewpoints. As employees advance to higher levels in the organization, they will need to solve problems and make difficult decisions, and this session will give them the confidence to know that they have made the best decisions possible.

Whether a formal business letter, a print advertisement, or an informal email, the written word is often the only exposure customers have to a business. "Business Writing" not only helps employees review the proper use of grammar and sentence structure, but it also addresses the latest concerns of business communications. Those concerns include shorter attention spans, surplus information, and the constantly urgent status of many activities. As a result, it is even more important to get the point across using accuracy, brevity, and clarity. This session outlines methods to organize documents and addresses the important concept of tone and its role in business writing. In addition, as email is quickly becoming the prevalent method of communication today, a section of the course is devoted to successful email practices.

An understanding of business skills and processes needn't be reserved for senior management or high-level executives. A broader understanding of business processes helps employees become strategic thinkers who can visualize more readily what opportunities are available for growth. This opens the door for advanced career mapping and development of employees, creating the basis for succession planning efforts for organizations. "Basic Business Knowledge" guides learners through the maze of business terms and cycles, allowing them to comprehend their organization's role in the global marketplace. The study of financial concepts and business math allows learners to analyze financial statements and understand their significance to the organization's bottom line.

What Are the Ultimate Outcomes?

These courses create employees who better understand their place in the organization and how their daily actions make a difference in its goals and success. This creates a stronger workforce with more potential for advancement as the opportunities arise.

Priority Management 14

What's in This Chapter?

- Objectives for the half-day workshop
- Lists of materials for facilitator and participants
- Detailed program agenda to be used as a facilitator's guide

▲   ▲   ▲

This session on priority management encompasses methods to organize the various components of an employee's day. Those components include scheduling, projects, and records. In addition, this module looks at the challenges that make organizing those components difficult and offers procedures to overcome them to create a more balanced and effective workday.

The half-day workshop enables attendees to participate in either discussion or practice of managing priorities, and the exercises can be adjusted to allow more in-depth practice if time is available. At the end of the workshop, learners will commit to action items for continued development.

Training Objectives

The participants' objectives for the half-day priority management workshop are to be able to

- set goals and create action plans to achieve those goals
- employ time management practices to prioritize and accomplish tasks
- establish a plan for continued development of priority management skills.

⊙ ✖ Materials

For the facilitator:

- this chapter, for reference and use as a facilitator guide
- Learning Activity 14-1: Introductions
- Learning Activity 14-2: Self-Assessment
  - ○ Assessment 14-1: Self-Assessment
- Learning Activity 14-3: Mastering Your Time
- Learning Activity 14-4: Time Management Practice
  - ○ Training Instrument 14-1: Time Management Tasks
  - ○ Training Instrument 14-2: Prioritization Chart
- Learning Activity 14-5: Project Management
  - ○ Training Instrument 14-3: Project Management Chart
- Learning Activity 14-6: Managing Records
- Learning Activity 14-7: Problem Paper
  - ○ Training Instrument 14-4: Paperwork Samples
- Learning Activity 14-8: Putting It All Together
- Assessment 14-2: Program Evaluation
- PowerPoint slide program, titled "Priority Management" (slides 14-1 through 14-41). To access slides for this program, open the file *UBBB_PowerPointSlides_Ch14.ppt* on the accompanying CD. Thumbnail versions of the slides for this workshop are included at the end of this chapter.
- projector, screen, and computer to display slides
- flipchart and markers.

For the participants:

- pens or pencils for each participant
- name badge for each participant
- set of handouts for each participant
- sticky notes attached to the front of each set of handouts
- assorted toys and puzzles for the participant tables
- snacks and candy as desired.

Sample Agenda

START	ACTIVITY	MINUTES
:00	Welcome	:05
:05	Objectives and Agenda	:05
:10	Introductions (14-1)	:15
:25	Self-Assessment (14-2)	:20
:45	Mastering Your Time (14-3)	:20
1:05	Time Management Practice (14-4)	:45
1:50	Break	:15
2:05	Project Management (14-5)	:25
2:30	Managing Records (14-6)	:20
2:50	Problem Paper (14-7)	:45
3:35	Putting It All Together (14-8)	:15
3:50	Closing	:10

8:00 a.m. Welcome (5 minutes)

 As participants enter the room, display **slide 14-1** on the screen, to greet your learners. Welcome them and introduce yourself. Explain that the purpose of the workshop is to help them make the best use of their time by focusing on the tasks that make a difference and organizing and managing the projects, resources, and records involved in their daily activities.

You can expand upon this discussion to include any specific themes of your organization being addressed by the workshop, such as new technologies or adjusted processes. In addition, this is a good time to mention that the participants may already use some of the practices that will be discussed today, so this can serve as a refresher for them. Finally, impress upon them that this session is an important opportunity to share their expertise in priority management practices that have worked well for them.

Rules

Explain the ground rules for the session. Here are some sample ground rules and housekeeping items:

- Turn cell phones to silent. (Turn off your own phone first, to lead by example and to ensure that your phone isn't the one that rings during the session.)

- This workshop is interactive. The most important things the participants will learn from this class are the ideas and suggestions that are shared by their fellow learners. They should be prepared to contribute to the discussions. (You can even use small prizes or other incentives to increase their participation in the session.)

- A break is scheduled during the session.

- Restrooms, smoking areas, snacks, and vending machines are located in the following areas: *[add details]*.

- Respectful communication is required. If someone is speaking, please give that person your complete attention.

🕐 8:05   Objectives and Agenda (5 minutes)

PPT Present **slide 14-2** and review the workshop objectives. The participants should understand that in today's session we will focus our efforts on the activities that really matter.

PPT Go through the agenda items listed on **slide 14-3** and ask for any questions.

🕐 8:10   Introductions (15 minutes)

PPT Show **slide 14-4** to set the stage for introductions, and explain that you want everyone to meet each other. Tell the participants that you'd also like to help them get an overview of the types of issues they have in common with others in the room. Use **learning activity 14-1** to help identify these issues.

🕐 8:25   Self-Assessment (20 minutes)

PPT Show **slide 14-5** and conduct **learning activity 14-2** to help the participants narrow down which areas of priority management they should focus on today to get the best results from this session.

🕐 8:45   Mastering Your Time (20 minutes)

PPT Show **slide 14-6** and discuss the importance of assigning priorities to roles and responsibilities at work and at home. What's the difference between managing time and mastering time? Invite the participants to take a look at these concepts in **learning activity 14-3**, using **slides 14-7 through 14-19** as illustrations.

🕐 9:05   Time Management Practice (45 minutes)

PPT Show **slide 14-20**, and use **learning activity 14-4** to give the participants an opportunity to practice the techniques they've just studied. Until this point, the participants have looked at steps to help them with individual planning. When others are involved in planning, the steps are similar but a little more involved. That's when project management concepts can help coordinate activities. The learners will discover those when they return from their break.

🕐 9:50   Break (15 minutes)

10:05 **Project Management** (25 minutes)

 Show **slide 14-21** to introduce project management. Conduct **learning activity 14-5**, using **slides 14-22 through 14-25** to help the participants generate a project management plan that uses a structured, step-by-step process.

 10:30 **Managing Records** (20 minutes)

 Show **slide 14-26** to introduce the segment on records management. No matter what the size of a project, it's always a challenge to keep up with the documents and papers that are attached to it. That's the challenge that **learning activity 14-6** addresses. Use this learning activity, as well as the strategies outlined in **slides 14-27 through 14-37**, to find ways to meet this challenge.

 10:50 **Problem Paper** (45 minutes)

Use **learning activity 14-7** as a way to demonstrate to the learners the effectiveness of handling paperwork efficiently.

Remind the participants that no learning experience is successful unless you take the time to come up with an action plan to put the information to use.

 11:35 **Putting It All Together** (15 minutes)

 Show **slide 14-38** to indicate that it is time to summarize what has been learned in today's session. Conduct **learning activity 14-8** with **slides 14-39 and 14-40** to summarize the objectives the participants have learned and to review a one-day, one-week, and one-month action plan for putting the skills into practice after the workshop to continue developing their priority management skills.

 11:50 **Closing** (10 minutes)

Display **slide 14-41** as a way to close the workshop, and point out that your contact information is listed on the slide, in case the learners think of additional questions once they get back to the workplace. Remind the participants that managing their priorities ensures that they're doing the right things to get the outcomes they need. Ask them which tools they picked up today might help them retain and build upon their priority management skills. Emphasize that these are the insights you'd like them to remember as they go back to their departments.

Explain to the participants that you, too, want to continue to develop your skills, and that they can help you by filling out an evaluation form to let you know what they liked or what changes they would like to see. Distribute **assessment 14-2**, ask the learners to complete it, and point out where they can leave the forms when they exit the room.

Thank the learners for their attention, and end the workshop with a motivating story, quote, or anecdote from your personal collection.

 12:00 p.m.   Adjourn

 What to Do Next

- Using the material in this chapter as a guide, build a detailed plan to prepare for this workshop.

- To adjust the length of this session, add more discussion time to the section on mastering your time to include a more involved study of time wasters and some potential solutions; add a practice session to the section on Project Management; and expand the section concerning time wasters with discussion of specific challenges that are being experienced by the participants.

- Schedule a training room and invite your attendees. To build interest, options may include changing the title of the session to a catchy tie-in to your industry or business, sending an introductory email that includes common priority management concerns in your organization, or doing presentations in individual departmental meetings.

- Draft a supply list, teaching notes, and time estimates. If you'd like to customize your teaching notes, print the slides as note pages and add them to your own outline to ensure that you don't omit any key points.

- Decide how you will support the action plan to which your learners will commit. If you determine that you want to customize the action plan on **slide 14-40** for your organization, get input from participating department managers as to which items they would like to act upon.

- Consider designing follow-up sessions to encourage the learners to continue to develop priority management skills.

- For additional modules, background information, and extended training sessions on this subject, refer to the resources used in the development of these materials, specifically, *Time Management Training,* by Lisa J. Downs (ASTD Press, 2008) and *Manager Skills Training* by Christee Gabour Atwood (ASTD Press, 2008).

PowerPoint Slides

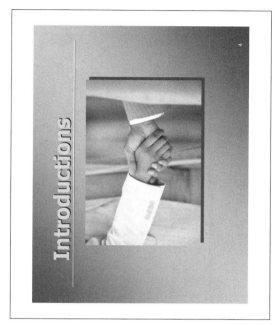

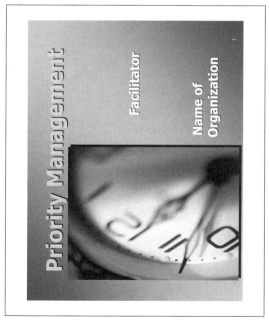

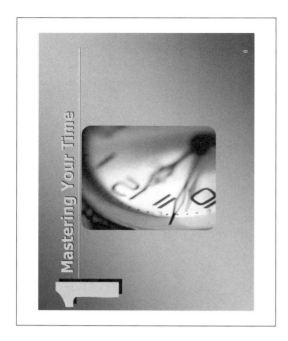

Mastering Your Time

Step 1: Prioritizing

- Focus on roles and responsibilities at work and at home
- Ask yourself, "What is the most important thing for me to be doing at this time?"
- Devote less energy to non-critical tasks
- Know what your work actually is and what is involved.

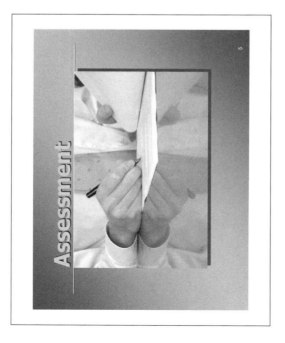

Assessment

Needs Fulfilled by Time Management

- To feel more in control of our lives
- To make the most of every day
- To accomplish what we set out to do

Step 2: Analyzing

- Look closely at where you are spending your time
- Log your time for one week
- Search for pockets of time, items to cut, time of day tasks are done, pace of work
- Analyze and adjust scheduling and routines as needed.

10

Step 3: Filtering

- We cannot find time; we have to make it by taking it away from other activities.
- The easiest option is not always the best.
- Consider if the action is what you want or need to be doing right now; if not, say "no."

12

Model for Reviewing Work

- 50,000+ feet: Life as a whole
- 40,000 feet: 3-5 year vision
- 30,000 feet: 1-2 year goals
- 20,000 feet: Areas of responsibility
- 10,000 feet: Current projects
- Ground level: Current actions

Source: Allen, David. Getting Things Done. New York, NY: Penguin Group, 2001.

9

Questions to Ask

- How are most of your hours spent?
- Is your schedule in balance (work, family, time for self)?
- Did anything from your log surprise you?
- Is there any time you cannot account for?
- How do you decide what to spend your time doing?

11

Step 4: Scheduling

- Creates a plan of action for days, weeks, months.
- Uses organizational tools: planner, PDA, scheduling software, lists.
- Assists with focus on important tasks and responsibilities aligned with priorities.
- Allows for flexibility as needs change.

14

Scheduling Tips

- Do important tasks first.
- Break large tasks down into pieces.
- Schedule for long-term and short-term.
- Build in breaks for yourself.
- Be ready to "let it go" if necessary; not all days will go according to plan.

16

Filtering Categories

- Urgent / Important: Needs immediate attention Aligns with priorities
- Important / Not Urgent: No sense of immediacy Must be done
- Urgent / Not Important: Not tied to priorities Involves others' urgencies
- Not Important Not Urgent: Time wasters

Source: Cook, Marshall J. Time Management. Avon, MA: Adams Media, 1998. 13

Scheduling Tips

- Record to-do items in one reliable location.
- Overestimate time to accomplish tasks.
- Avoid overbooking to allow for interruptions and urgencies.
- Keep things in perspective.
- Customize your format and be flexible.

Source: Allen, David. Getting Things Done. New York, NY: Penguin Group, 2001. 15

Executing "Saying No"

- Meetings are ineffective or unnecessary.
- New projects are misaligned with goals or resources.
- Tasks are a waste of time; look for alternative actions.
- You are not the right person for the job.
- You need to focus.

Time Management Exercise

Step 5: Execute

- Take action based on plans and priorities.
- Take charge of your time and your schedule.
- Acknowledge when and where time wasters occur and take steps to eliminate.
- Use goals, roles, and responsibilities to drive productivity.

Self Management

- Time cannot be saved or stored.
- We must manage ourselves in relation to time.
- It's the way we use time that matters, not how much we have.
- Any bad habits must be changed to better control our use of time.

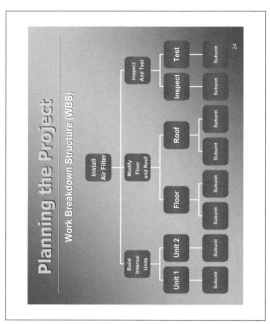

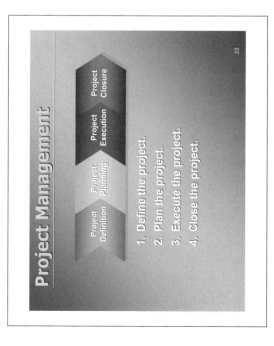

Managing Records

3

Our Sources of Clutter

- Nesting instinct: Things provide a sense of security and comfort.
- Messy = creative: In reality, a mess is costing you time.
- Chronic saving: You never know when you might need it.

Project Management

Action	Deadline	Responsible	Resources	Notes
Always starts with a verb	Must be completed by:	Who will do this?	What is needed? What can help with this task?	What needs to happen first? Other notes.

Tracking
Symbols
✓ Complete
✗ Delete
IP In Progress

Questions to Ask Yourself

- Can I really find what I need quickly and can someone else find it if necessary?
- Is my work environment slowing me down or making me feel out of control?
- Do I feel overwhelmed by paper?

1. Sort

- If overwhelming, start with small chunks of time: 15 minutes, 30 minutes, and so forth.
- Stand up while sorting; this increases efficiency with sense of urgency.
- Touch each item only one and make a quick decision.

30

Notes on Filing Documents

- Keep hanging file tabs on one side of the folder only for easy scanning.
- Create different file folders: reading, to-do, vendors, invoices, upcoming events, and so forth; store them in a wire rack for easy access.

32

The Paperwork Process

- Step 1: Sort items into categories.
- Step 2: Take action: file, delegate, or toss.
- Step 3: Maintain a paperwork routine.

29

2. Take Action

- If a piece of paper only needs a brief response, do it now.
- Schedule a short filing session once a day, week, or month.
- If a more thoughtful response is required, schedule a task.

31

Tips to Handle Paperwork

- Carry a notebook with you at all time to present having loose pieces of paper.
- Create files immediately and keep an accessible file cabinet close.
- Keep supplies for rerouting and recycling handy.

34

Tips to Handle Paperwork

- Ask "How valuable is this information?"
- Toss envelopes right away.
- Toss old drafts of documents.
- Throw out the previous month's magazine when the new one arrives.

36

3. Maintain a Routine

- Block out time for dealing with clutter 15 minutes a day, one hour a week, and so forth.
- Use files, containers, and other desk accessories for easy organization.
- Ask, "Do I really want or need this?"

33

Tips to Handle Paperwork

- Ask to be taken off of unnecessary mailing lists and subscriptions.
- Clip useful material from periodicals and toss the rest.
- Skim and scan reading material; schedule reading for twice a week.

35

5 Putting It All Together

38

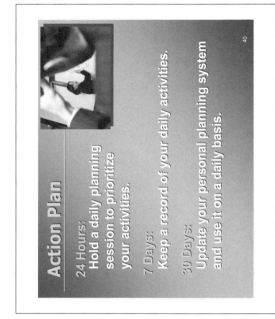

Action Plan

24 Hours;
Hold a daily planning session to prioritize your activities.

7 Days:
Keep a record of your daily activities.

30 Days:
Update your personal planning system and use it on a daily basis.

40

Tips to Handle Paperwork

- Ask subordinates to limit the number and length of written reports.

- Cut back on sending and keeping memos; call instead.

- Enter business contacts into a database; toss business cards when done.

37

Summary

Our objectives today were to learn to

- ✧ identify methods to analyze and organize tasks

- ✧ apply basic project management concepts

- ✧ demonstrate techniques to arrange and reduce paper records and files.

39

Decision Making and Problem Solving 15

What's in This Chapter?

- Objectives for the half-day workshop

- Lists of materials for facilitator and participants

- Detailed program agenda to be used as a facilitator's guide

▲   ▲   ▲

Effective decision-making and problem-solving skills require taking into consideration all important factors, weighing benefits, and determining solutions that will lead to the desired outcome. In this session, learners will have an opportunity to practice a standardized process to make the best decisions possible.

The half-day workshop enables attendees to participate in either discussion or practice of skills for each topic included, and the activities can be adjusted to allow more in-depth practice, if time is available. At the end of the workshop, learners will commit to action items for continued development.

Training Objectives

The participants' objectives for the half-day decision-making workshop are to be able to

- evaluate factors and make the best decisions based on the information available

- use the steps of problem solving to resolve challenges

- establish a plan for continued development of decision-making skills.

⊙ ✖ **Materials**

For the facilitator:

- this chapter, for reference and use as a facilitator guide
- Learning Activity 15-1: Introductions
- Learning Activity 15-2: Self-Assessment
  - Assessment 15-1: Self-Assessment
- Learning Activity 15-3: The Five D's of Decision Making
  - Training Instrument 15-1: Decision-Making Instruments
- Learning Activity 15-4: Decision-Making Practice
- Learning Activity 15-5: Problem Solving
  - Training Instrument 15-2: The Steps of Problem Solving
- Learning Activity 15-6: STEM—System, Training, Environment, and Motivation
- Learning Activity 15-7: Problem-Solving Activity
  - Training Instrument 15-3: Problem-Solving Practice
- Learning Activity 15-8: Putting It All Together
- Assessment 15-2: Program Evaluation
- PowerPoint slide program, titled "Decision Making and Problem Solving" (slides 15-1 through 15-30). To access slides for this program, open the file *UBBB_PowerPointSlides_Ch15.ppt* on the accompanying CD. Thumbnail versions of the slides for this workshop are included at the end of this chapter.
- projector, screen, and computer to display slides
- flipchart and markers.

For the participants:

- pens or pencils for each participant
- name badge for each participant
- set of handouts for each participant
- sticky notes attached to the front of each set of handouts
- assorted toys and puzzles for the participant tables
- snacks and candy as desired.

⏰ Sample Agenda

START	ACTIVITY	MINUTES
:00	Welcome	:05
:05	Objectives and Agenda	:05
:10	Introductions (15-1)	:15
:25	Self-Assessment (15-2)	:20
:45	The 5 D's of Decision Making (15-3)	:25
1:10	Decision-Making Practice (15-4)	:45
1:55	Break	:15
2:10	Problem Solving (15-5)	:25
2:35	STEM (15-6)	:15
2:50	Problem-Solving Activity (15-7)	:45
3:35	Putting It All Together (15-8)	:15
3:50	Closing	:10

⏰ 8:00 a.m.   Welcome (5 minutes)

 As participants enter the room, display **slide 15-1** to greet your learners. Welcome them and introduce yourself. Explain that the purpose of the workshop is to practice methods that will help them make better decisions and to weigh options to come up with effective solutions to the problems they face each day.

To help the learners concentrate on this workshop, explain that you are offering them the opportunity to leave their problems at the door. Write "Problems" on a flipchart page, and tell the participants to use a sticky note to write a general problem that is waiting for them back at their offices. They can use any problem they can think of, as long as they don't use names and they don't mind if it is used in an example during the problem-solving process later in the session.

You can expand your introduction to include any specific themes of your organization being addressed by the workshop. The workshop can also remind the learners of some of the steps of problem solving they might have forgotten. Finally, impress upon the participants that this session is an important opportunity to share their expertise and practices that have worked well for them.

Rules

Explain the ground rules for the session. Here are some sample ground rules and housekeeping items:

- Turn cell phones to silent. (Turn off your own cell phone to lead by example and ensure that your phone isn't the one that rings during the session.)

- This workshop is interactive. The most important things the participants will learn from this class are the ideas and suggestions shared by their fellow learners. They should be prepared to contribute to the discussion. (You can even use small prizes or other incentives to increase their participation in the session.)

- A break is scheduled during the session.

- Restrooms, smoking areas, snacks, and vending machines are located in the following areas: *[add details]*.

- Respectful communication is required. If someone is speaking, please give that person your complete attention.

8:05   Objectives and Agenda (5 minutes)

PPT Show **slide 15-2,** and review the workshop objectives on the slide. The participants should understand that today's session focuses on all possibilities for answers to our decisions or problems, and it determines which one is the best for our desired outcome.

PPT Go through the agenda items on **slide 15-3** and ask your learners if they have any questions.

8:10   Introductions (15 minutes)

 To begin this segment, display **slide 15-4** and explain that you want everyone to meet each other. Tell them that you'd also like them to think about their challenges in making effective decisions. Conduct **learning activity 15-1** with **slide 14-5** to help the learners get to know one another and to determine the learners' biggest challenges in decision making and problem solving.

8:25   Self-Assessment (20 minutes)

 Show **slide 15-6**, which introduces the concept of assessment. Then use **learning activity 15-2** to help the learners assess the areas in which they can strengthen their decisions and problem-solving skills.

8:45   The Five D's of Decision Making (25 minutes)

PPT Show **slide 15-7** to begin this section on decision making. Give a general introduction on the benefits of good decision-making skills, using personal examples or current events for an illustration of the importance of developing these skills.

 As in any other workplace skill, people can practice and improve their ability to make decisions. Conduct **learning activity 15-3**, with **slides 15-8 through 15-15**, to allow learners to practice the steps of decision making and to learn about various methods that can help them make informed decisions.

9:10   Decision-Making Practice (45 minutes)

 Show **slide 15-16.** Introduce **learning activity 15-4** by explaining that the best way to learn any new process is to have an opportunity to practice it immediately. That's what they'll do in this learning activity.

Remind the learners that although some of their choices are single decisions, other decisions require problem-solving skills before they can get to the ultimate decision-making stage. The next section will address those skills.

 9:55   Break (15 minutes)

 10:10   Problem Solving (25 minutes)

 Present **slide 15-17** to introduce the concept of problem solving and the benefits of using a standardized system to gather and evaluate potential solutions. Conduct **learning activity 15-5** with **slides 15-18 through 15-23** to walk learners through the steps of problem solving.

Learners will need to determine whether the problem is the issue they are trying to solve or whether the issue is just a symptom of a bigger problem. The next section will give the learners some techniques to make that determination.

 10:35   STEM—System, Training, Environment, and Motivation (15 minutes)

 Show the headline on **slide 15-24** to begin **learning activity 15-6**, which helps learners distinguish between a system and the problem. **Slides 15-24 and 15-25** explain this method and the acronym STEM (System, Training, Environment, and Motivation). Once learners have had an opportunity to think about the problem-solving "big picture," it's time to practice on an individual situation.

 10:50   Problem-Solving Activity (45 minutes)

 Show the headline of **slide 15-26** to introduce the problem-solving activity. Conduct **learning activity 15-7** to practice the steps of solving a workplace challenge.

 11:35   Putting It All Together (15 minutes)

 Show **slide 15-27** and remind participants that no learning experience is successful unless they take the time to come up with an action plan to put the information to use. Conduct **learning activity 15-8** to help the participants review all the information from this workshop. **Slides 15-28 and 15-29** summarize the objectives covered in this workshop and include a one-day, one-week, and one-month action plan.

⏰ 11:50 Closing (10 minutes)

PPT Show **slide 15-30**. Note that your contact information is listed on the slide, in case the learners come up with additional questions when they get back to their office.

Close the session by asking which of the tools they picked up today might help them to make better decisions and resolve their problems more effectively. Tell the learners that these are the insights you'd like them to remember as they go back to their departments.

 Remind the participants that you, too, want to continue to develop your skills and that they can help you by filling out an evaluation form to let you know what they liked about the session or what changes they would like to see made. Distribute **assessment 15-2**, and ask the learners to complete it. Point out where they can leave the forms when they exit the room.

Thank the learners for their attention and end with a motivating story, quote, or anecdote from your personal collection.

⏰ 12:00 p.m. Adjourn

◆ What to Do Next

- Using the material in this chapter as a guide, build a detailed plan to prepare for this workshop.

- To adjust the length of this session, add more discussion time to the section on problem solving, add a specific decision submitted by a participant to be taken through the process, or add another round of structured experiences to the decision practice.

- Schedule a training room and invite your attendees. To build interest, options may include changing the title of the session to a catchy tie-in to your industry or business, sending an introductory email that includes common decision-making concerns in your organization, or doing presentations in individual departmental meetings.

- Draft a supply list, teaching notes, and time estimates. If you'd like to customize your teaching notes, print the slides as note pages and add your own outline to ensure you don't omit any key points.

- Decide how you will support the action plan to which your learners will commit. If you determine that you want to customize the action plan on **slide 15-29** to your organization, get input from participating department managers on what items they would like included as action items.

- Consider designing follow-up sessions or reinforcement emails to encourage the learners to continue to develop decision-making skills.

- For additional modules, background information, and extended training sessions on this subject, refer to the resources used in the development of these materials, specifically *Leadership Training* by Lou Russell (ASTD Press, 2003), *Manager Skills Training* by Christee Gabour Atwood (ASTD Press, 2008), and *Teamwork Training* by Sharon Boller (ASTD Press, 2005).

PowerPoint Slide

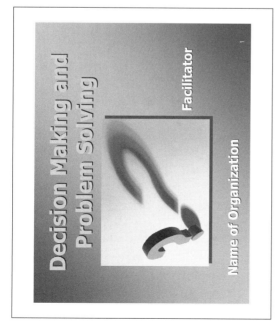

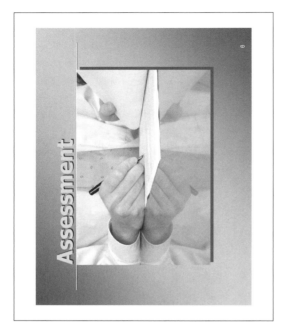

Decision Making

2 Determine Desired Outcome

If you were to find the perfect solution to this situation, what would it do?

10

4 Decide Best Solution

GROUP METHODS
Best of Two
Dot System
Brainwriting
9-Block Grid
Other Ideas?

12

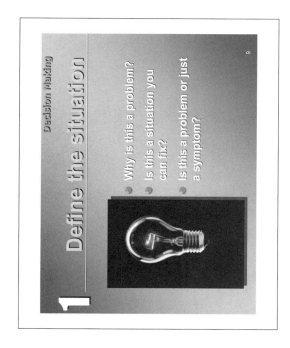

Decision Making

1 Define the situation

● Why is this a problem?

● Is this a situation you can fix?

● Is this a problem or just a symptom?

9

3 Discover Alternatives

Research should consider

✓ realistic

✓ resources

✓ risk

✓ results

11

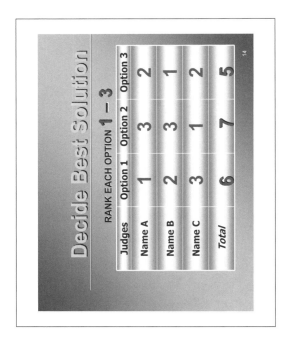

Decide Best Solution

RANK EACH OPTION 1 – 3

Judges	Option 1	Option 2	Option 3
Name A	1	3	2
Name B	2	3	1
Name C	3	1	2
Total	6	7	5

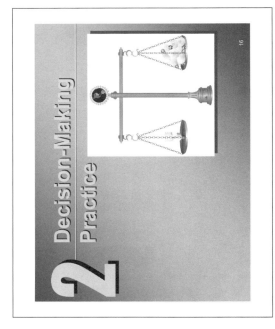

Decision-Making

Practice

2

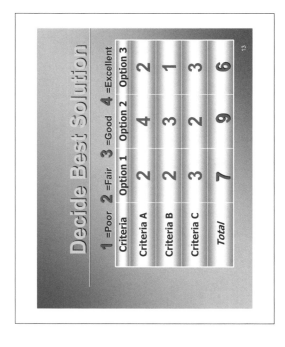

Decide Best Solution

1 =Poor   2 =Fair   3 =Good   4 =Excellent

Criteria	Option 1	Option 2	Option 3
Criteria A	2	4	2
Criteria B	2	3	1
Criteria C	3	2	3
Total	7	9	6

Do It!

✓ Create an action plan.
✓ Determine responsibility for each step.
✓ Follow up to ensure follow-through.
✓ Evaluate and revise as needed.
✓ Record lessons learned.

5

Problem-Solving Steps

5. Verify the solution

Ask if the solution is acceptable, and summarize agreements.

22

What is the Difference Between a Symptom and a Problem?

SYMPTOM:

❖ "The payroll checks are all wrong!"

PROBLEM?

❖ The direct users don't know how to use the system.

❖ There is a bug in the calculation program.

❖ The printer is jamming on the checks.

24

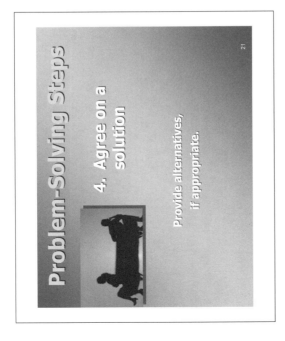

Problem-Solving Steps

4. Agree on a solution

Provide alternatives, if appropriate.

21

Problem-Solving Steps

6. Follow up

Do what you say you will do.

23

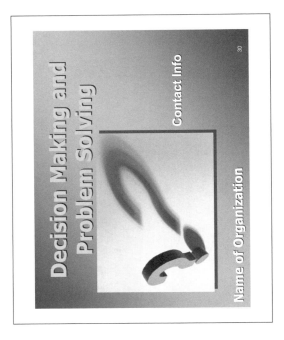

Business Writing and Email 16

What's in This Chapter?

- Objectives for the half-day business writing workshop

- Lists of materials for facilitator and participants

- Detailed program agenda to be used as a facilitator's guide

▲   ▲   ▲

Written communications can present a professional image of an organization if they encompass the rules of grammar, business writing techniques, and a touch of public relations. In this session, learners will refresh their understanding of basic grammar principles and have an opportunity to practice their writing skills with commonly used documents and emails.

The half-day workshop enables attendees to participate in either discussion or practice of the skills of each topic included, and the exercises can be adjusted to allow more in-depth practice if time is available. At the end of the workshop, learners will commit to action items for continued development.

Training Objectives

The participants' objectives for the half-day workshop are to be able to

- demonstrate the principles of professional and accurate business documents

- use basic guidelines for effective email communications.

⊙ ✖ Materials

For the facilitator:

- this chapter, for reference and use as a facilitator guide
- Learning Activity 16-1: Introductions
- Learning Activity 16-2: Business Writing Checkup
  - Assessment 16-1: Self-Assessment
- Learning Activity 16-3: Business Writing Overview
  - Training Instrument 16-1: Business Writing Basics
- Learning Activity 16-4: Organization of Documents
  - Training Instrument 16-2: Document Planning Form
  - Training Instrument 16-3: Try It Out
- Learning Activity 16-5: Grammar and Tone
- Learning Activity 16-6: Email Guidelines
- Learning Activity 16-7: Frequently Used Documents
  - Training Instrument 16-4: Frequently Used Documents
- Learning Activity 16-8: Putting It All Together
- Assessment 16-2: Program Evaluation
- PowerPoint slide program, titled "Business Writing and Email" (slides 16-1 through 16-47). To access slides for this program, open the file *UBBB_PowerPointSlides_Ch16.ppt* on the accompanying CD. Thumbnail versions of the slides for this workshop are included at the end of this chapter.
- projector, screen, and computer to display slides
- flipchart and markers.

For the participants:

- pens or pencils for each participant
- name badge for each participant
- set of handouts for each participant
- sticky notes attached to the front of each set of handouts
- assorted toys and puzzles for the participant tables
- snacks and candy as desired.

🕐 Sample Agenda

START	ACTIVITY	MINUTES
:00	Welcome	:05
:05	Objectives and Agenda	:05
:10	Introductions (16-1)	:15
:25	Business Writing Checkup (16-2)	:30
:55	Business Writing Overview (16-3)	:25
1:20	Organization of Documents (16-4)	:30
1:50	Break	:15
2:05	Grammar and Tone (16-5)	:25
2:30	Email Guidelines (16-6)	:25
2:55	Frequently Used Documents (16-7)	:40
3:35	Putting It All Together (16-8)	:15
3:50	Closing	:10

🕐 8:00 a.m. Welcome (5 minutes)

 As participants enter the room, present **slide 16-1** to greet them. Welcome everyone and introduce yourself. Ask the learners what they think when they receive a letter from a company that contains a number of errors or is worded in a confusing manner. That's the impression the participants can give to others if they don't pay attention to the written words they send out—whether in a formal letter, report, or quickly sent email. Explain that the purpose of the workshop is to refresh us on the principles of effective writing and to remind us of the importance of using those principles in every document we create.

You can expand on this discussion to include specific themes of your organization being addressed during the workshop. The workshop can also remind the participants of some of the grammar rules they might have forgotten.

Rules

Explain the ground rules for the session. Here are some sample rules and housekeeping items:

- Turn cell phones to silent. (Turn your own cell phone off first, to lead by example and ensure that your phone isn't the one that rings during the session.)

- This workshop is interactive. The most important things the participants will learn from this class are the ideas and suggestions shared by their fellow learners. They should be prepared to contribute to the discussions. (You can even use small prizes or other incentives to increase their participation in the session.)

- A break is scheduled during the session.

- Restrooms, smoking areas, snacks, and vending machines are located in the following areas: *[add details].*

- Respectful communication is required. If someone is speaking, please give that person your complete attention.

8:05 Objectives and Agenda (5 minutes)

Show **slide 16-2** and review the workshop objectives from the slide. The learners should understand that today's session is designed to help us ensure that every document we send gives a professional impression.

Show **slide 16-3**, go through the agenda items, and ask for any questions.

8:10 Introductions (15 minutes)

Show **slide 16-4** to set the stage for the introductions to follow. Explain that you want everyone to meet each other and start to look at some of our biggest grammar challenges. Use **learning activity 16-1** as a way for the participants to meet the other members of the workshop and, at the same time, help them realize the number of grammar and writing errors we encounter every day.

8:25 Business Writing Checkup (30 minutes)

Slide 16-5 introduces the learners to the idea of assessment. In **learning activity 16-2**, the participants will get a chance to assess their knowledge of grammar and to see which grammar rules they've forgotten since their school days. Remind the learners that they shouldn't feel bad if they didn't get all of the questions correct on the assessment. That's why business writing classes are so important for all of us. Even skilled writers lose track of those grammar rules, and with "spell-check" available on computers, our spelling skills have diminished even further!

8:55 Business Writing Overview (25 minutes)

Show **slide 16-6** to begin an overview of business writing basics. Conduct **learning activity 16-3** with **slides 16-7 through 16-10** to relate some of the most important points of written business communications.

9:20 Organization of Documents (30 minutes)

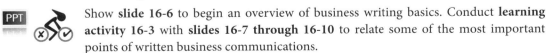
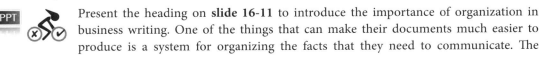

Present the heading on **slide 16-11** to introduce the importance of organization in business writing. One of the things that can make their documents much easier to produce is a system for organizing the facts that they need to communicate. The participants will find a formula for that process as you conduct **learning activity 16-4** and show **slides 16-11 through 16-15**.

Two areas that can make a big difference in the way a document is received are grammar and tone. That's the area the participants will investigate when they return from their break.

9:50   Break (15 minutes)

10:05   Grammar and Tone (25 minutes)

Show **slide 16-16** to introduce the ideas of grammar and tone. Even the most effectively organized documents can give the wrong impression, depending on the grammar and tone of the communication. Conduct **learning activity 16-5** with **slides 16-17 through 16-28** to demonstrate proper standards of grammar and appropriate tone for business communications.

For a smooth transition to the next activity, tell the participants that you are about to look at one of the most abused forms of business writing. Ask them if they can guess what it is.

10:30   Email Guidelines (25 minutes)

Show **slide 16-29** to begin the section about email, and conduct **learning activity 16-6** with **slides 16-30 through 16-35** to let the learners practice applying some of these email guidelines to create effective and positive email messages.

Tell the learners that now they'll have an opportunity to look at some of the other common documents they use frequently.

10:55   Frequently Used Documents (40 minutes)

Show **slide 16-36** to introduce this section. Use **learning activity 16-7** to review the standards and practices for frequently used documents as outlined on **slides 16-37 through 16-43**.

11:35   Putting It All Together (15 minutes)

Remind the participants that their learning experience will not be successful unless they take the time to come up with an action plan to put the information to use. **Slide 16-44** emphasizes that it is time to put all the information together. Conduct **learning activity 16-8** with **slide 16-45** for a summary of the objectives covered in this workshop, and **slide 16-46** to encourage the learners to think about how they can implement the one-day, one-week, and one-month plan to continue to develop their business writing skills.

11:50   Closing (10 minutes)

Show **slide 16-47**. Note that your contact information is listed on the slide, in case participants think of additional questions when they return to the workplace.

Close the session by briefly discussing what a big impression writing makes on their customers. Ask the learners which of the tools they picked up today might help them to present a more professional image in their writing. Suggest that these are the insights you'd like them to remember as they go back to their departments.

 Remind the participants that you want to continue to develop your skills, too, and that they can help you by filling out an evaluation form to let you know what they liked about the session or what changes they would like to see. Distribute **assessment 16-2**, ask the learners to complete it, and indicate where they can leave the forms when they exit the room.

Thank the learners for their attention, and end with a motivating story, quote, or anecdote from your personal collection.

12:00 p.m.   Adjourn

What to Do Next

- Using the material in this chapter as a guide, build a detailed plan to prepare for this workshop.

- To adjust the length of this session, add more discussion time to the overview of business writing, or add another round of writing samples after each topic is discussed, so participants can make adjustments and see whether they have improved their writing skills.

- Schedule a training room and invite your attendees. To build interest, options may include changing the title of the session to a catchy tie-in to your industry or business, sending an introductory email that includes the benefits of effective written communication, or doing presentations in individual departmental meetings.

- Draft a supply list, teaching notes, and time estimates. If you'd like to customize your teaching notes, print the slides as note pages and add your own outline to ensure that you don't omit any key points.

- Decide how you will support the action plan to which your learners will commit. If you determine that you want to customize the action plan on **slide 16-46** to your organization, get input from participating department managers about which items they would like to include as action items.

- Consider designing follow-up sessions or emails with helpful hints to encourage the learners to continue to develop business writing skills.

- For additional modules, background information, and extended training sessions on this subject, refer to the resources used in the development of these materials, specifically *Manager Skills Training* by Christee Gabour Atwood (ASTD Press, 2008) and *10 Steps to Successful Business Writing* by Jack Appleman (ASTD Press, 2008).

PowerPoint Slides

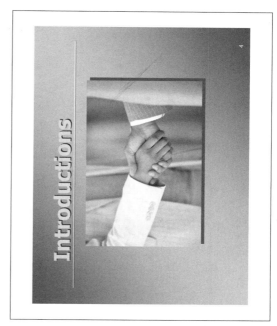

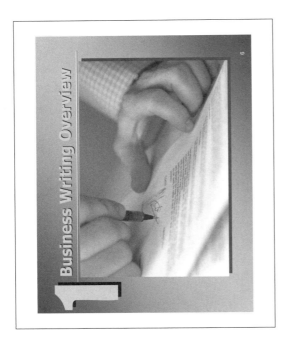

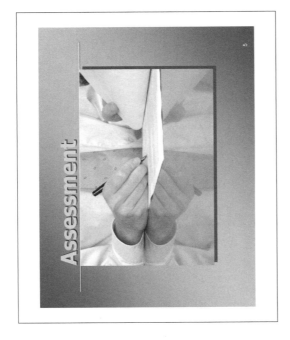

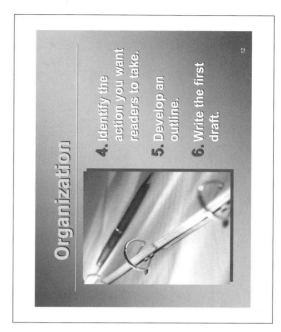

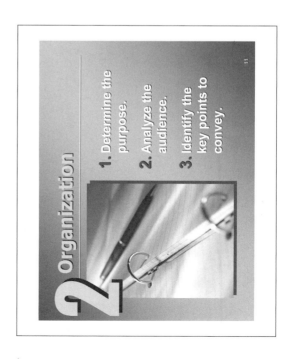

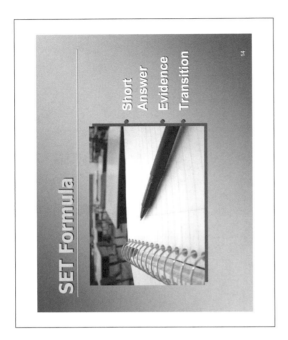

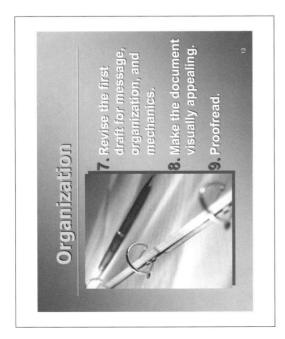

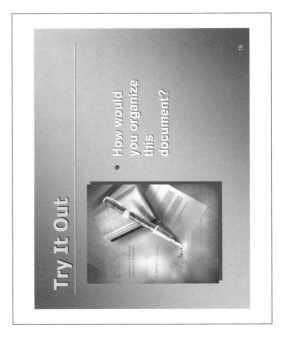

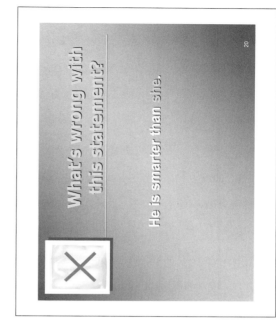

Email Guidelines

- Use bullets and headings to make it easier for readers to read the email quickly.

34

Frequently Used Documents

36

Email Guidelines

- Cut and paste if possible instead of hitting the reply button. It's easy to send a message accidentally before you're ready.

33

Email Guidelines

- Save informal language and abbreviations (lol, btw) for your personal emails.

35

Document Standards

- Use subject lines, headings, and openings as advertisements so people will want to read your communications.

Document Standards

- Review every document not only for grammar and spelling, but also for tone and appropriate language.

Document Standards

- Create templates for documents you use frequently, such as emails, memos, reports, and letters.

Document Standards

- Partner with another person to be proofreaders for each other's documents.
- Never send major documents without at least two proofreaders' review.

Document Standards

- Leave out buzzwords and acronyms that your audience might not understand.

42

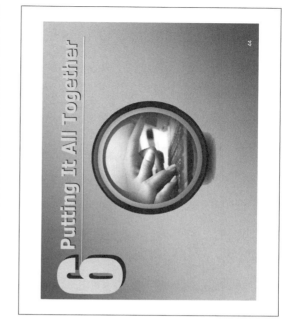

6

Putting It All Together

44

Document Standards

- Use basic language that will be clear to your audience.
- Edit documents so they contain the smallest number of words that will convey your point.

41

Document Standards

- Don't use documents for communications that should be done one-on-one.

43

Action Plan

24 Hours:
Review a document for errors and tone.

7 Days:
Enlist the aid of a proofreader for your important documents.

30 Days:
Create a template for one of your frequently used documents.

46

Business Writing and Email

Contact Info

Name of Organization

47

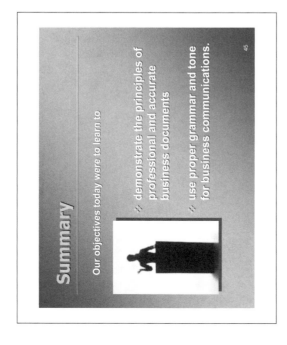

Summary

Our objectives today were to learn to

❖ demonstrate the principles of professional and accurate business documents

❖ use proper grammar and tone for business communications.

45

Basic Business Knowledge 17

What's in This Chapter?

- Objectives for the half-day business knowledge workshop
- Lists of materials for facilitator and participants
- Detailed program agenda to be used as a facilitator's guide

▲   ▲   ▲

Comprehension of basic business principles is required for any employee to better understand the influence that his or her individual role plays on organizational success. In this session on basic business knowledge, learners will study business terminology, cycles, and basic financial concepts to better understand the organization and strategic thinking. In addition, this workshop includes an exciting opportunity to help attendees understand the current objectives of the organization by having departmental representatives or senior executives act as panelists and resources.

You will need to contact leaders of your organization and get their commitment to be a part of this program. Scheduling will be a consideration to ensure that they will be able to be present for their segments. This workshop enables attendees to learn from these individuals to understand the overall vision and operation of the organization. Your guest speakers will participate in one of two sections of the program: the company overview at the beginning of the session or the business operations section near the end of the program. For a well-rounded workshop, invite a representative of the executive team for the overview and an operations officer or financial representative for the business operations portion.

If the individuals are available, you may also want to consider including a panel discussion among a number of leadership representatives on their areas of operation.

This workshop presents an invaluable opportunity for members of your organization to understand their larger role in the company and to have the rare opportunity to interact with leadership executives.

Training Objectives

The participants' objectives for the half-day workshop are to be able to

- develop an understanding of the organization's goals and operations

- define basic business terms and financial concepts

- establish a plan for continued development of business knowledge skills.

Materials

For the facilitator:

- this chapter, for reference and use as a facilitator guide

- Learning Activity 17-1: Introductions

  ○ Training Instrument 17-1: Introductions

- Learning Activity 17-2: Self-Assessment

  ○ Assessment 17-1: Self-Assessment

- Learning Activity 17-3: Company Overview

  ○ Training Instrument 17-2: Company Overview

- Learning Activity 17-4: Basic Business Knowledge

  ○ Training Instrument 17-3: Basic Business Knowledge

- Learning Activity 17-5: Business Financials

  ○ Training Instrument 17-4: Business Financial Terms

- Learning Activity 17-6: Business Operations

  ○ Training Instrument 17-5: Business Operations

- Learning Activity 17-7: Putting It All Together

- Assessment 17-2: Program Evaluation

- PowerPoint slide program, titled "Basic Business Knowledge" (slides 17-1 through 17-21). To access slides for this program, open the file *UBBB_PowerPointSlides_Ch17.ppt* on the accompanying CD. Thumbnail versions of the slides for this workshop are included at the end of this chapter.

- projector, screen, and computer to display slides

- flipchart and markers.

For the participants:

- pens or pencils for each participant
- name badge for each participant
- set of handouts for each participant
- sticky notes attached to the front of each set of handouts
- assorted toys and puzzles for the participant tables
- snacks and candy as desired.

 ## Sample Agenda

START	ACTIVITY	MINUTES
:00	Welcome	:05
:05	Objectives and Agenda	:05
:10	Introductions (17-1)	:20
:30	Self-Assessment (17-2)	:20
:50	Company Overview (17-3)	:45
1:35	Basic Business Knowledge (17-4)	:35
2:10	Break	:15
2:25	Business Financials (17-5)	:25
2:50	Business Operations (17-6)	:45
3:35	Putting It All Together (17-7)	:15
3:50	Closing	:10

 ## 8:00 a.m.   Welcome (5 minutes)

PPT As participants enter the room, display **slide 17-1** as a greeting to your learners. Welcome them and introduce yourself. Explain that the purpose of the workshop is to give the participants an overview of the business principles and terminology that will help them understand the big picture of business and the organization.

You can expand on this discussion to include any specific themes of your organization being addressed by the workshop.

Rules

Explain the ground rules for the session. Here are some sample rules and housekeeping items:

- Turn cell phones to silent. (Turn off your own cell phone first, to lead by example and ensure that your phone isn't the one that rings during the session.)

- This workshop is interactive. The most important things the participants will take away from this class are the ideas and suggestions shared by their fellow learners. They should be prepared to contribute to the discussions. (You can even use small prizes or other incentives to increase their participation in the session.)

- A break is scheduled during the session.

- Restrooms, smoking areas, snacks, and vending machines are located in the following areas: *[add details]*.

- Respectful communication is required. If someone is speaking, please give all of your attention to that person.

 8:05   Objectives and Agenda (5 minutes)

 Show **slide 17-2** and review the workshop objectives. The learners should understand that today's session is designed to provide a "big picture" view that will help us as we grow in our positions in the organization.

 Present the agenda items on **slide 17-3**, and ask for any questions.

 8:10   Introductions (20 minutes)

 Display **slide 17-4** to set the stage for the introductions to follow. Explain that you want everyone to meet each other and get an understanding of where each person fits into the business picture. Conduct **learning activity 17-1** to help the participants get comfortable with one another and to help them recognize the specific business skills of the group.

 8:30   Self-Assessment (20 minutes)

 Show **slide 17-5** to set the stage for assessment. Conduct **learning activity 17-2** to see which areas they can learn more about in today's session.

At this point, a leader in your organization will give the group the "view from 50,000 feet," also known as "the big picture."

 8:50   Company Overview (45 minutes)

 Show **slide 17-6** and conduct **learning activity 17-3** with corresponding **slides 17-7 through 17-11** to help participants analyze the vision, mission, and current trends of the organization.

Ask the learners to relate some of the business terms or concepts they hear around the office that may confuse them. You can list these on a flipchart to add to the discussion in the next segment.

 9:35   Basic Business Knowledge (35 minutes)

 Show **slide 17-12**, which is an introduction to the company vision and mission. Use **learning activity 17-4** and **slide 17-13** to familiarize the participants with the basic business concepts that will allow them to have a broader view of their organization as a business.

 10:10   Break (15 minutes)

 10:25   Business Financials (25 minutes)

 Present **slide 17-14** to open the section on business financials. Showing **slide 17-15**, conduct **learning activity 17-5**, so the learners get a chance to understand the bottom line of business as they analyze financial reports. Explain to the learners that the next activity will give them a chance to practice the techniques they've discussed today by using their new business knowledge in their own company.

 10:50   Business Operations (45 minutes)

 Present **slide 17-16** to introduce this last portion of the workshop. Showing **slide 17-17**, use **learning activity 17-6** to help learners analyze and practice basic business operations.

Remind the learners that no learning experience is successful unless you take the time to come up with an action plan to put the information learned to use.

 11:35   Putting It All Together (15 minutes)

 Slide 17-18 indicates that it's time for a summary of today's session. Conduct **learning activity 17-7** with **slide 17-19** to confirm that you have covered the objectives together and show **slide 17-20** with an action plan to follow for one day, one week, and one month.

 11:50   Closing (10 minutes)

Display **slide 17-21** and point out that your contact information is listed on the slide, in case the learners come up with additional questions when they get back into the workplace.

Close the session by briefly discussing how basic business knowledge will help the learners in their daily activities. Ask the learners which of the tools they picked up today will help them more fully understand the big picture of the organization. Suggest that these are the insights you'd like them to remember as they go back to their departments.

 Remind the learners that you, too, want to continue to develop your skills and that they can help you by filling out an evaluation form to let you know what they liked about the session or what changes they would like to see made. Distribute **assessment 17-2**, ask the learners complete it, and indicate where they can leave the forms when they exit the room.

Thank the participants for their attention, and end with a motivating story, quote, or anecdote from your personal collection.

 ## 12:00 p.m.   Adjourn

 ## What to Do Next

- Using the material in this chapter as a guide, build a detailed plan to prepare for this workshop.

- To adjust the length of this session, add more discussion time to the section on business cycles, or add a question-and-answer session with managers or upper-level executives, so participants have an opportunity to get the latest information about the business processes of the organization.

- Schedule a training room and invite your attendees. To build interest, options may include changing the title of the session to a catchy tie-in to your industry or business, sending an introductory email that includes the importance of having basic business knowledge, or doing presentations in individual departmental meetings.

- Draft a supply list, teaching notes, and time estimates. If you'd like to customize your teaching notes, print the slides as note pages and add your own outline to ensure that you don't omit any key points.

- Decide how you will support the action plan to which your learners will commit. If you determine that you want to customize the action plan on **slide 17-20** to your organization, get input from participating department managers on what items they would like to include for action.

- Consider designing follow-up sessions or update emails to encourage the learners to continue to develop their understanding of business and their organization.

- For additional modules, background information, and extended training sessions on this subject, refer to the resources used in the development of these materials, specifically *Sales Training* by Jim Mikula (ASTD Press, 2003) and *Manager Skills Training* by Christee Gabour Atwood (ASTD Press, 2008).

PowerPoint Slides

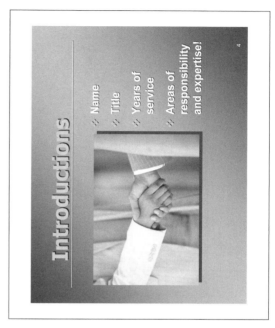

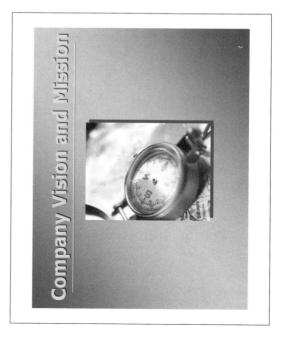

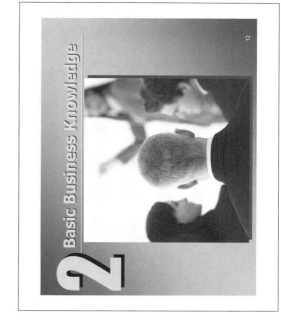

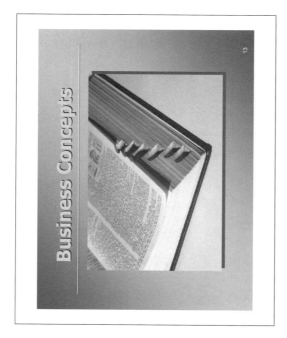

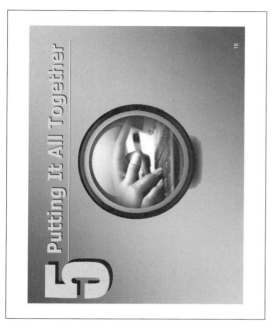

5 Putting It All Together
18

Action Plan

24 Hours:
Share something you learned about the organization with others in your department.

7 Days:
Analyze items in the news that relate to business knowledge concepts.

30 Days:
Write a report for your manager reviewing the highlights of the this session.

20

Your Company Name Here

Using your business plan worksheet, your group will

❖ answer the questions to determine your company's business plan

❖ prepare a presentation to introduce your company to the rest of the class.

17

Summary

Our objectives today were to learn to

❖ develop an understanding of the organization's goals and operations

❖ define basic business terms and financial concepts

❖ establish a plan for continued development of business knowledge skills.

19

Section Five:
Professionalism

Professionalism Overview 18

What's in This Section?

- Professional Image
- Social Skills and Basic Etiquette
- Working in Teams
- Work-Life Balance
- Professional Development

▲ ▲ ▲

Even employees with superior work skills can continue to develop by focusing on the courses offered in this section on professionalism. The study of topics that extend beyond the employees' specific job responsibilities can create a lasting influence on their daily actions.

The development of a broader understanding of professionalism and the importance of interacting productively with others in teams and social settings creates well-rounded employees. In addition, methods adapted to retain a sense of balance develop a stronger foundation for life both in the workplace and outside it.

What's in Each Module?

The module "Professional Image" addresses much more than outward appearance. It investigates the deeper values involved in creating the professional presence, including the three A's: attitude, actions, and accountability. In this workshop, learners will have an opportunity to focus on these issues and the standards of business ethics and values. Shaping stronger employees from the inside out is the goal of this seminar.

The module "Social Skills and Basic Etiquette" goes beyond the dilemma of determining the right utensil to use in formal dining situations. This session includes attributing the proper respect and titles, developing confidence in social situations, and building a level of rapport that creates mutually beneficial relationships. The session also addresses the accepted use of technology in social interactions.

In the module "Working in Teams," learners study the personality traits and communication styles of team members so they can work more productively with others. It examines team processes that help new groups evolve into unified teams more quickly. It also assesses methods to ensure that goals are met and results evaluated. As a result, each team activity becomes a lesson to build on for future endeavors.

Burnout and turnover are common issues in today's business world, and the time spent in the module "Work-Life Balance" will allow participants to evaluate their levels of satisfaction or stress to achieve the right balance. They will study their professional and personal goals so they can work toward a better quality of life both on and off the job. The participants will also practice turning goals into action plans. The final segment will introduce methods of stress management to help them retain perspective.

Superior employees are characterized by an enduring desire for continued learning and development. In the "Professional Development" module, we have addressed this desire by creating a set of professional goals, studying the competencies required for that advancement, and formulating an individual development plan to achieve those goals. This session creates an opportunity to identify the future leaders of an organization as they design their individual plans for development, identify potential mentors, and prioritize their next steps.

What Are the Ultimate Outcomes?

Professionalism is sometimes considered that indefinable *it* that a few select individuals possess. Organizations that carefully cultivate an understanding of the concepts taught in this series can develop a higher level of professionalism in members of their workforce who might have otherwise been overlooked.

Professional Image 19

What's in This Chapter?

- Objectives for the half-day professional image workshop

- Lists of materials for facilitator and participants

- Detailed program agenda to be used as a facilitator's guide

▲   ▲   ▲

This session on professional image addresses the three areas that define professional behavior: attitude, accountability, and actions. Learners will assess their current level of professionalism and focus on those areas in which development is needed. Other topics addressed in this workshop include standards of business ethics, decision making, and conflict resolution.

The half-day workshop enables attendees to participate in either discussion or practice of the skills of each topic included, and the exercises can be adjusted to allow more in-depth practice, if time is available. At the end of the workshop, learners will commit to action items for continued development.

Training Objectives

The participants' objectives for the half-day professional image workshop are to be able to

- assess their professionalism and areas for development

- identify and exemplify professionalism in appearance, behaviors, and activities.

⊙ ✖ Materials

For the facilitator:

- this chapter, for reference and use as a facilitator guide
- Learning Activity 19-1: Introductions
- Learning Activity 19-2: Self-Assessment
  - ○ Assessment 19-1: Self-Assessment
- Learning Activity 19-3: Professionalism Overview
- Learning Activity 19-4: The Attitude of Professionalism
  - ○ Training Instrument 19-1: Professionalism Indicators
- Learning Activity 19-5: Accountability of Professionals
  - ○ Training Instrument 19-2: Accountability in Difficult Situations
- Learning Activity 19-6: Professionalism in Difficult Situations
- Learning Activity 19-7: Professionalism in Action
  - ○ Training Instrument 19-3: Professionalism Development Plan
- Learning Activity 19-8: Putting It All Together
- Assessment 19-2: Program Evaluation
- PowerPoint slide program, titled "Professional Image" (slides 19-1 through 19-21). To access slides for this program, open the file *UBBB_PowerPointSlides_Ch19.ppt* on the accompanying CD. Thumbnail versions of the slides for this workshop are included at the end of this chapter.
- projector, screen, and computer to display slides
- flipchart and markers.

For the participants:

- pens or pencils for each participant
- name badge for each participant
- set of handouts for each participant
- sticky notes attached to the front of each set of handouts
- assorted toys and puzzles for the participant tables
- snacks and candy as desired.

⏰ Sample Agenda

START	ACTIVITY	MINUTES
:00	Welcome	:05
:05	Objectives and Agenda	:05
:10	Introductions (19-1)	:15
:25	Self-Assessment (19-2)	:20
:45	Professionalism Overview (19-3)	:25
1:10	The Attitude of Professionalism (19-4)	:35
1:45	Break	:15
2:00	Accountability of Professionals (19-5)	:35
2:35	Professionalism in Difficult Situations (19-6)	:35
3:10	Professionalism in Action (19-7)	:25
3:35	Putting It All Together (19-8)	:15
3:50	Closing	:10

⏰ 8:00 a.m.   Welcome (5 minutes)

 As participants enter the room, display **slide 19-1** to greet your learners. Welcome them and introduce yourself. Explain that the purpose of the workshop is to give them an overview of professionalism and how it can affect their activities and their careers. You can expand on this discussion to include any specific themes of your organization addressed by the workshop.

Rules

Explain the ground rules for the session. Here are some sample rules and housekeeping items:

- Turn cell phones to silent. (Turn off your own cell phone first, to lead by example and ensure that your phone isn't the one that rings during the session.)

- This workshop is interactive. The most important things the participants will take away from this class are the ideas and suggestions shared by their fellow learners. They should be prepared to contribute to the discussions. (You can even use small prizes or other incentives to increase their participation in the session.)

- A break is scheduled during the session.

- Restrooms, smoking areas, snacks, and vending machines are located in the following areas: *[add details]*.

- Respectful communication is required. If someone is speaking, please give that person your complete attention.

8:05   Objectives and Agenda (5 minutes)

Show **slide 19-2** and review the workshop objectives. The participants should understand that today's session is designed to emphasize the importance of a professional image and discuss how we can improve our own.

Review the agenda items on **slide 19-3**, and ask for any questions.

8:10   Introductions (15 minutes)

Show **slide 19-4** to set the stage for introductions. Explain that you want everyone to meet each other and get a snapshot of what's included in professional image. Use **learning activity 19-1** to help the learners recognize the specific traits that signify professional behavior.

8:25   Self-Assessment (20 minutes)

Display **slide 19-5** to introduce the concept of assessment. Conduct **learning activity 19-2** to give the learners a chance to assess their areas of strength and weakness in the development of their professional image. This will indicate areas on which they need to concentrate in today's workshop.

8:45   Professionalism Overview (25 minutes)

Show **slide 19-6** to begin the discussion about how we perceive professionals and which traits they exhibit. Note that many topics come under the heading of *image*. Use **learning activity 19-3** and **slide 19-7** to help learners recognize the traits of professionalism.

9:10   The Attitude of Professionalism (35 minutes)

Show **slide 19-8**. The behaviors and traits of professionals described in the overview all begin with an attitude of professionalism. This concept is introduced via the three indicators discussed as you conduct **learning activity 19-4** with **slides 19-9 through 19-12**.

Professional individuals are those who take responsibility for their actions, are ethical in the decisions they make, and are consistent in their approach to difficult situations. The learners will investigate these areas further after the break.

9:45   Break (15 minutes)

10:00   Accountability of Professionals (35 minutes)

Discuss professional accountability as introduced in **slide 19-13**. Conduct **learning activity 19-5** to analyze the standards of ethics and responsibilities of professionals.

10:35   Professionalism in Difficult Situations (35 minutes)

Show **slide 19-15**. Another aspect of the accountability of professionalism shows up in the way individuals handle themselves in difficult situations. Decision making and conflict resolution are two of the areas the learners will practice in **learning activity 19-6**.

  11:10   Professionalism in Action (25 minutes)

Display **slide 19-16** to introduce *professionalism in action*. Conduct **learning activity 19-7** with **slide 19-17** to give learners a chance to think about the way their actions reinforce their professionalism.

 11:35   Putting It All Together (15 minutes)

Present **slide 19-18** to begin to wrap up the workshop. Remind them that no learning experience is successful unless people take the time to come up with an action plan to put the information to use.

 Conduct **learning activity 19-8**, using **slides 19-19 and 19-20** to summarize how the session has addressed its objectives and to create a plan to continue to develop the learners' professional images.

 11:50   Closing (10 minutes)

Display **slide 19-21** and note that your contact information is listed on the slide, in case the learners come up with additional questions when they return to the workplace.

Close the session by briefly discussing how professionalism can affect the participants' career paths. Ask which of the tools they picked up today will help them understand the importance of professionalism and give them ways to bring it into their workplace. Suggest that these are the insights you'd like them to remember as they go back into their departments.

 Remind the learners that you, too, want to continue to develop your skills and that they can help you by filling out an evaluation form to let you know what they liked in the session or what changes they would like to see. Distribute **assessment 19-2**, ask the learners to complete it, and indicate where they can leave the forms when they exit the room.

Thank the learners for their attention, and end with a motivating story, quote, or anecdote from your personal collection.

12:00 p.m.   Adjourn

What to Do Next

• Using the material in this chapter as a guide, build a detailed plan to prepare for this workshop.

- To adjust the length of this session, add more discussion time to the section on ethics and values, or add a question-and-answer session with managers so participants have an opportunity to get a feel for the professionalism issues that are most important to the organization.

- Schedule a training room and invite your attendees. To build interest, options may include changing the title of the session to a catchy tie-in to your industry or business, sending an introductory email, or doing presentations in individual departmental meetings.

- Draft a supply list, teaching notes, and time estimates. If you'd like to customize your teaching notes, print the slides as note pages and add your own outline to ensure you don't omit any key points.

- Decide how you will support the action plan to which your learners will commit. If you determine that you want to customize the action plan on **slide 19-20** to your organization, get input from participating department managers on which items they would like to include for action.

- Consider designing follow-up sessions or update emails to encourage each learner to continue to develop his or her professional image.

- For additional modules, background information, and extended training sessions on this subject, refer to the resources used in the development of these materials, specifically *Manager Skills Training* by Christee Gabour Atwood (ASTD Press, 2008) and *Developing Great Managers* by Lisa Haneberg (ASTD Press, 2008).

PowerPoint Slides

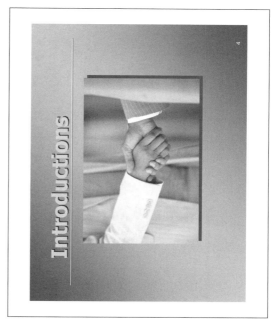

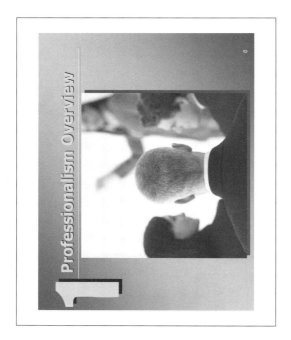

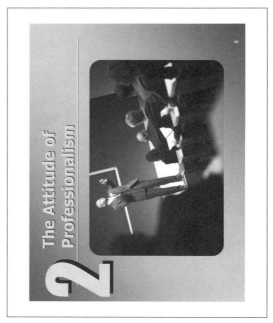

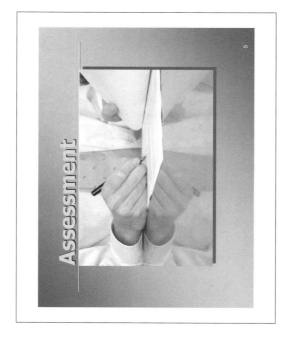

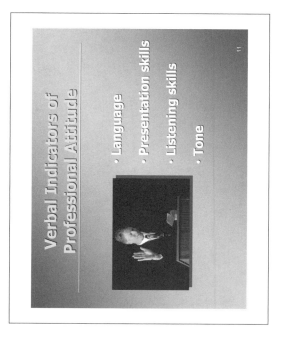

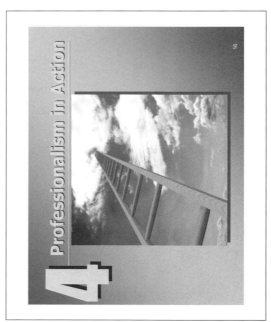

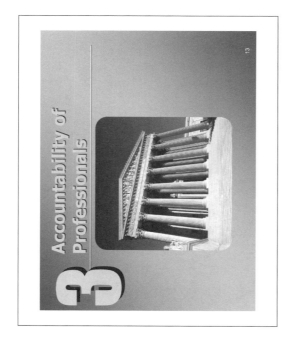

5 Putting It All Together

18

Action Plan

24 Hours:
Determine one area of professionalism to develop.

7 Days:
Implement one action for development of that area.

30 Days:
Assess progress and determine next steps for development.

20

Professionalism in Action

- How do your actions support your values, your vision, your attitude, and your accountability?

- What is your plan to develop your level of professionalism?

17

Summary

Our objectives today were to be able to

- assess professional behaviors and areas for development

- identify professionalism in appearance, behaviors, and activities.

19

Social Skills and Basic Etiquette $\quad$ 20

What's in This Chapter?

- Objectives for the half-day social skills workshop

- Lists of materials for facilitator and participants

- Detailed program agenda to be used as a facilitator's guide

The half-day workshop allows learners to practice the skills that will help them create a positive impression in social and business interactions. The sophistication and self-confidence that come from knowing the proper methods of interaction are only part of the benefit of studying business etiquette. In addition, the study of etiquette and proper social behavior can help in networking, effective communication, and the respectful interaction with others of various backgrounds and positions.

On the other hand, improper etiquette can be a negative influence and even a deal-breaker in business situations. This session allows learners the opportunity to study and practice the basics of effective social and business interactions.

Training Objectives

The participants' objectives for the half-day workshop are to be able to

- perform proper introductions

- interact appropriately in social situations

- use correct protocol at business meals and meetings.

◎ ✖ **Materials**

For the facilitator:

- this chapter, for reference and use as a facilitator guide
- Learning Activity 20-1: Introductions
- Learning Activity 20-2: Self-Assessment
  - ◦ Assessment 20-1: Self-Assessment
- Learning Activity 20-3: Social Skills Overview
- Learning Activity 20-4: Culture Shock
  - ◦ Training Instrument 20-1: Culture Shock
- Learning Activity 20-5: Business Etiquette
  - ◦ Training Instrument 20-2: Business Etiquette Checklist
- Learning Activity 20-6: Social Settings
  - ◦ Training Instrument 20-3: Social Attire Chart
- Learning Activity 20-7: Dining
- Learning Activity 20-8: Communications Etiquette
- Learning Activity 20-9: Putting It All Together
- Assessment 20-2: Program Evaluation
- PowerPoint slide program, titled "Social Skills and Basic Etiquette" (slides 20-1 through 20-32). To access slides for this program, open the file *UBBB_PowerPointSlides_Ch20.ppt* on the accompanying CD. Thumbnail versions of the slides for this workshop are included at the end of this chapter.
- projector, screen, and computer to display slides; alternatively, overhead transparencies and overhead projector
- flipchart and markers.

For the participants:

- pens or pencils for each participant
- name badge for each participant
- set of handouts for each participant
- sticky notes attached to the front of each set of handouts

- assorted toys and puzzles for the participant tables

- snacks and candy as desired.

🕐 Sample Agenda

Start	Activity	Minutes
:00	Welcome	:05
:05	Objectives and Agenda	:05
:10	Introductions (20-1)	:15
:25	Introductions IQ (20-2)	:20
:45	Social Skills Overview (20-3)	:25
1:10	Culture Shock (20-4)	:40
1:50	Break	:15
2:05	Business Etiquette (20-5)	:25
2:30	Social Settings (20-6)	:20
2:50	Dining (20-7)	:25
3:15	Communications Etiquette (20-8)	:20
3:35	Putting It All Together (20-9)	:15
3:50	Closing	:10

The times assigned to the elements of this training are approximate and will vary with discussion and facilitator emphasis.

Before the class begins, set the room with these items:

- PowerPoint slide 20-1

- posted agenda for the day

- binder with participants' handouts at each seat

- sticky notes attached to each binder

- pencils or pens

- blank paper for each participant

- name badge for each participant

- assorted snacks and candies, as desired.

🕐 8:00 a.m. Welcome (5 minutes)

[PPT] Display **slide 20-1** to greet your learners. Welcome the participants and introduce yourself. Explain that the purpose of the workshop is to help them to navigate any social situation with self-confidence and appropriate behavior. You can note that they are already using many of the practices that will be discussed today, and this can be a refresher course for them. It will also serve as an update for some of the differences in culture that might affect how they interact with others.

Rules

Explain the ground rules for the session. Here are some sample ground rules and housekeeping items:

- Turn cell phones to silent. (Turn your own cell phone off to lead by example and ensure that your phone isn't the one that rings during the session.) Also remind the learners that making sure that electronic devices are silenced and refraining from "texting" during business and social situations is a sign of respect to others in the room.

- This workshop is interactive. The most important things participants take away from this class are the ideas and suggestions their fellow learners share. Be prepared to participate!

- A break is scheduled during the session.

- Restrooms, smoking areas, snacks, and vending machines are located in the following areas: *[add details]*.

- Respectful communication is required. If someone is speaking, please give that person your complete attention.

🕐 8:05 Objectives and Agenda (5 minutes)

[PPT] Present **slide 20-2** and review the workshop objectives shown on the slide. The learners should understand that the focus of today's session is to recognize the social customs that show respect toward those with whom they interact in business.

[PPT] Go through the agenda items on **slide 20-3**, and ask if there are any questions.

🕐 8:10 Introductions (15 minutes)

[PPT] Display **slide 20-4** to set the stage for the introductions that will follow. The learners will have a chance to become comfortable in their learning environment and to practice their social skills in **learning activity 20-1**.

These introductions and the discussion set the stage for the following assessment of their knowledge of introduction etiquette

🕐 8:25 Introductions IQ (20 minutes)

[PPT] Show **slide 20-5** to signal to the learners that it's time for an assessment of their knowledge of introduction etiquette.

Introductions are just the opening to the world of social skills. The gestures, body language, conversation topics, and attention to details of different cultures are all part of the social skills and business etiquette that can make a difference in one's personal and professional image. Conduct **learning activity 20-2** using **slides 20-6 through 20-15** to establish etiquette guidelines for proper introductions.

8:45 Social Skills Overview (25 minutes)

 Present **slide 20-16** to introduce the overview of social skills and conduct **learning activity 20-3** with **slides 20-17 through 20-19** to help the learners analyze the benefits of paying attention to these skills. Emphasize that even when we think we're being very careful about our social skills, we can make mistakes. That's sometimes the case when we deal with people who have different backgrounds than ours, as in the next segment.

9:10 Culture Shock (40 minutes)

  Display **slide 20-20** to set the stage for the culture shock discussion. Use **learning activity 20-4** to help the learners recognize differences in nonverbal communication that exist between cultures, demonstrate the power of nonverbal communication, and build relationships among participants.

9:50 Break (15 minutes)

10:05 Business Etiquette (25 minutes)

  Display **slide 20-21** to introduce participants to business etiquette in different settings. Use **learning activity 20-5** and **slide 20-22** to help the learner determine practices that constitute appropriate behavior in business settings. This activity also outlines the basics of business cards, name tags, and other business etiquette items.

10:30 Social Settings (20 minutes)

  Although etiquette in business settings is important, our behavior in social settings is equally important. After displaying **slide 20-23** to introduce this section, discuss the basic guidelines for social settings as revealed in **learning activity 20-6** and **slide 20-24.**

10:50 Dining (25 minutes)

  Show **slide 20-25** to set the stage for dining, an area that many people find challenging. Conduct **learning activity 20-7** with **slides 20-25 and 20-26** to identify the parts of the formal place setting and to discuss proper dining practices.

The next section outlines some excellent guidelines to keep in mind when you use different forms of communications.

11:15 Communications Etiquette (20 minutes)

Show **slide 20-27** and note that good etiquette in both written and electronic communications can help build business relationships; it is a common courtesy that is often overlooked in today's fast-paced business climate. Conduct **learning activity 20-8** with **slide 20-28**, which will help the learner identify proper practices in written and electronic communications.

11:35 Putting It All Together (15 minutes)

Present **slide 20-29** to let the learner know that it's time to put together all the information they have learned. Conduct **learning activity 20-9** to create a plan for the learners to continue to develop their business etiquette and social skills. Remind the participants that no learning experience will be successful unless they take the time to come up with an action plan to put the information to use.

11:50 Closing (10 minutes)

Display **slide 20-32** to close the workshop. Note that your contact information is listed on the slide, in case they come up with additional questions after they've returned to the workplace. Close the session by briefly discussing how social skills can affect a person's career path. Ask the learners which of the tools that they picked up today will help them understand the importance of etiquette and find ways to bring it into their workplace. Suggest that these are the insights you'd like them to remember as they go back to their departments.

Finally, remind the participants that you, too, want to continue to develop your facilitation skills, just as they are developing their etiquette skills. Distribute **assessment 20-2** so they can give you their ideas for improvement on the final evaluation form. Ask them to complete the assessment and leave it in a designated spot before they leave.

Thank the learners for their attention, and end with a motivating or amusing story, quote, or anecdote from your collection.

12:20 p.m. Adjourn

What to Do Next

- Using the material in this chapter as a guide, build a detailed plan to prepare for this workshop.
- Schedule a training room and invite your attendees.
- Draft a supply list, teaching notes, and time estimates.
- Decide how you will support the action plan your learners will commit to.

- Consider designing follow-up sessions to encourage the learners to continue to develop social skills.

- For additional modules, background information, and extended training sessions on this subject, refer to the resources used in the development of these materials, specifically *Infoline* No. 250811, "Mind Your Business Manners," by Pamela Eyring (ASTD Press, November 2008) and *Listening Skills Training* by Lisa J. Downs (ASTD Press, 2008).

PowerPoint Slides

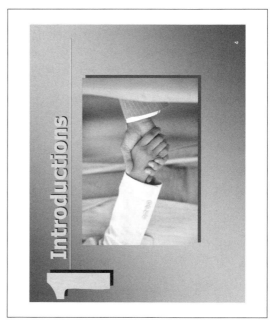

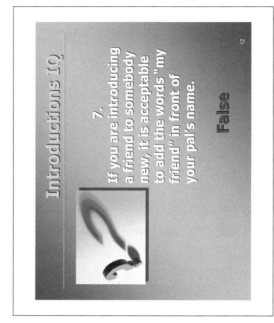

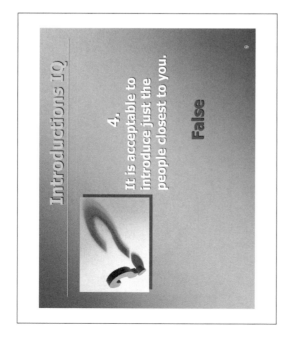

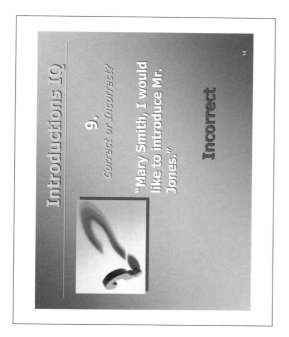

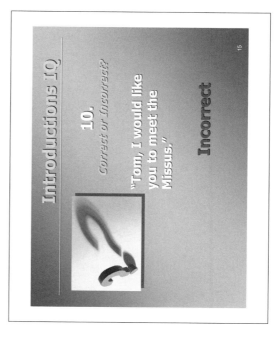

Business Etiquette

- ❖ Meetings and events
- ❖ Conferences
- ❖ Receptions
- ❖ Networking

22

Social Settings

Think about:

- ❖ Am I showing the proper respect?
- ❖ What social policies apply in this situation? (smoking, alcohol consumption, arrival and departure times, and so forth)
- ❖ Do I need to RSVP?
- ❖ What's the appropriate attire?
- ❖ What other factors could you consider?

24

3 Business Etiquette

21

4 Social Settings

23

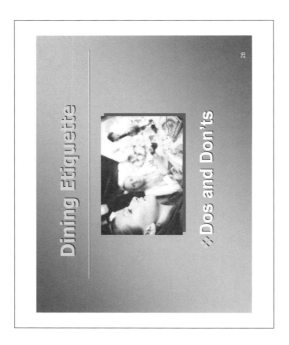

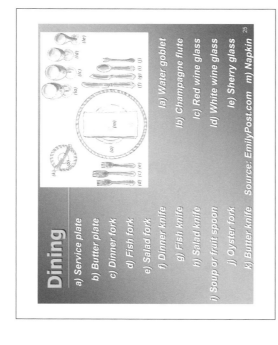

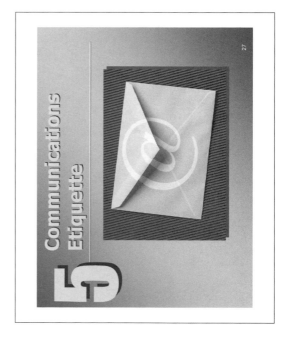

Summary

Our objectives today were to learn to

- perform proper introductions
- interact appropriately in social situations
- employ correct protocol at business meals and meetings.

30

Social Skills and Business Etiquette

Contact Info

Name of Organization

32

6 Putting It All Together

29

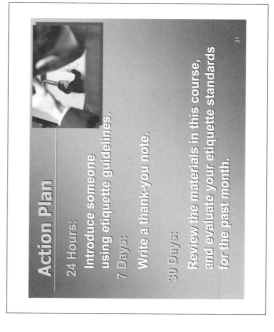

Action Plan

24 Hours:
Introduce someone using etiquette guidelines.

7 Days:
Write a thank-you note.

30 Days:
Review the materials in this course, and evaluate your etiquette standards for the past month.

31

Working in Teams 21

What's in This Chapter?

- Objectives for the half-day workshop

- Lists of materials for facilitator and participants

- Detailed program agenda to be used as a facilitator's guide

Every employee brings specific individual skills and abilities to the workplace. Equally important is an employee's ability to apply those skills effectively in a team situation. In this module, learners will assess their teamwork skills, analyze team dynamics, and study methods to encourage innovation in their teams.

The half-day workshop enables attendees to participate in either discussion or practice of the skills of each topic covered, and the activities can be adjusted to allow for more in-depth practice, if time is available. At the end of the workshop, learners will commit to action items for continued development.

Training Objectives

The participants' objectives for the half-day workshop are to be able to

- perform effectively as a member of a team

- communicate and interact with team members to achieve goals.

⊙ ⚒ Materials

For the facilitator:

- this chapter, for reference and use as a facilitator guide

- Learning Activity 21-1: Introductions

- Learning Activity 21-2: Self-Assessment

  ○ Assessment 21-1: Self-Assessment

- Learning Activity 21-3: Teamwork Overview

  ○ Training Instrument 21-1: Team Guidelines

- Learning Activity 21-4: Team Dynamics

  ○ Training Instrument 21-2: Creating Teams

- Learning Activity 21-5: Sabotage

  ○ Training Instrument 21-3: The Sabotage Exercise

  ○ Training Instrument 21-4: Sabotage Exercise Assignment Cards

- Learning Activity 21-6: Team Communications

  ○ Training Instrument 21-5: Team Listening Skills

  ○ Training Instrument 21-6: Team Meetings

- Learning Activity 21-7: Innovation and Creativity

  ○ Training Instrument 21-7: Brainstorming

- Learning Activity 21-8: Putting It All Together

- Assessment 21-2: Program Evaluation

- PowerPoint slide program, titled "Working in Teams" (slides 21-1 through 21-22). To access slides for this program, open the file *UBBB_PowerPointSlides_Ch21.ppt* on the accompanying CD. Thumbnail versions of the slides for this workshop are included at the end of this chapter.

- projector, screen, and computer to display slides

- flipchart and markers.

For the participants:

- pens or pencils for each participant

- name badge for each participant

- set of handouts for each participant

- sticky notes attached to the front of each set of handouts

- assorted toys and puzzles for the participant tables

- snacks and candy as desired.

🕐 Sample Agenda

START	ACTIVITY	MINUTES
:00	Welcome	:05
:05	Objectives and Agenda	:05
:10	Introductions (21-1)	:15
:25	Self-Assessment (21-2)	:20
:45	Teamwork Overview (21-3)	:20
1:05	Team Dynamics (21-4)	:45
1:50	Break	:15
2:05	Sabotage (21-5)	:30
2:35	Team Communications (21-6)	:35
3:10	Innovation and Creativity (21-7)	:25
3:35	Putting It All Together (21-8)	:15
3:50	Closing	:10

🕐 8:00 a.m.   Welcome (5 minutes)

PPT As participants enter the room, display **slide 21-1** as a greeting. Welcome them and introduce yourself. Explain that the purpose of the workshop is to give them an overview of teamwork and how they can make a difference in the performance of any team they join. You can expand on this discussion to include any specific themes of your organization being addressed by the workshop.

Rules

Explain the ground rules for the session. Here are some sample rules and housekeeping items:

- Turn cell phones to silent. (Turn off your phone first, to lead by example and ensure that your phone isn't the one that rings during the session.)

- This workshop is interactive. The most important things the participants will take away from this class are the ideas and suggestions shared by their fellow learners. They should be prepared to contribute to the discussions. (You can even use small prizes or other incentives to increase their participation in the session.)

- A break is scheduled during the session.

- Restrooms, smoking areas, snacks, and vending machines are located in the following areas: *[add details]*.

- Respectful communication is required. If someone is speaking, please give that person your complete attention.

🕐 8:05   Objectives and Agenda (5 minutes)

[PPT] Show **slide 21-2**, and review the workshop objectives from the slide. The learners should understand that today's session is designed to help create stronger teams that achieve their objectives and ideally create relationships among members that last beyond the duration of team activities. **[PPT]** Go through the agenda items on **slide 21-3** and ask for any questions.

🕐 8:10   Introductions (15 minutes)

[PPT] Present **slide 21-4** to set the stage for the introductions that will follow. Explain that you want everyone to meet each other and think about what it means to them to work in a team as well as what strengths they bring to their teams. Use **learning activity 21-1** as a way for the learners to become comfortable with each other as they get ready to learn about teamwork. The activity also helps them think about and identify the special skills that are useful to teams. The next activity will give the participants a chance to determine whether they are team players.

🕐 8:25   Self-Assessment (20 minutes)

[PPT] Show **slide 21-5** to introduce the concept of self-assessment. Conduct **learning activity 21-2** to help assess their areas of strength and potential development in their teamwork.

🕐 8:45   Teamwork Overview (20 minutes)

[PPT] Show **slide 21-6** and note that effective teams don't just happen. They result from planning and continual improvement. In the overview, the learners will look at the groundwork that makes a team become productive more quickly. Conduct **learning activity 21-3** while displaying **slide 21-7 through 21-9**, to introduce participants to the elements of effective teams.

🕐 9:05   Team Dynamics (45 minutes)

[PPT] Teams create synergy when diverse personalities, skills, and ideas work together to make the most of all members' abilities. Show **slide 21-10** to set the stage for team dynamics. Next, conduct **learning activity 21-4** to guide participants in learning how to help team members use their unique talents to support the team's mission.

🕐 **9:50   Break** (15 minutes)

🕐 **10:05   Sabotage** (30 minutes)

 Now the learners will discover what happens when someone on the team has a secret agenda. Tell them to look around. Someone in this room will be sabotaging their efforts. **Slide 21-11** shows four possible team personalities, and **slide 21-12** is a visual reminder of sabotage. Conduct **learning activity 21-5** so learners can discover how trust affects team behavior, as well as how it affects business productivity.

🕐 **10:35   Team Communications** (35 minutes)

Display **slide 21-13** to introduce the topic of team communications. Ask the participants if they've ever felt as though someone wanted to keep their team from fulfilling their mission. Explain that open, honest communication can prevent this. Conduct **learning activity 21-6** with **slides 21-14 through 21-16** to help participants learn to recognize teamwork communication skills and methods, as well as practice those skills.

🕐 **11:10   Innovation and Creativity** (25 minutes)

Show **slide 21-17** to set the stage for a session on innovation and creativity. Effective communications not only help the operations of a team, but they also create the foundation and trust that's needed for true innovative thinking and creativity. Conduct **learning activity 21-7** with **slide 21-18** to guide participants as they discover the difference creativity can make to their team and how to develop innovation in team members.

🕐 **11:35   Putting It All Together** (15 minutes)

Display **slide 21-19** to reinforce the idea that it's time to see how we can make practical use of the information presented in the workshop. Conduct **learning activity 21-8**, using **slides 12-20 and 12-21** to reinforce the learning objectives of the session and to create an action plan for continued development of their teamwork skills.

🕐 **11:50   Closing** (10 minutes)

Display **slide 21-22**, to indicate that the workshop is complete. Point out to the participants that your contact information is listed on the slide, in case they come up with additional questions after they've returned to the workplace.

Close the session by briefly discussing how their skills at working effectively as team members can affect the productivity of their departments. Ask the learners which of the tools they picked up today will help them understand the importance of teamwork and ways to create a better team environment in their workplaces. Suggest that these are the insights you'd like them to remember as they go back into their departments.

Remind the participants that you, too, want to continue to develop your skills and that they can help you by filling out an evaluation form to let you know what they liked about the session or what changes they would like to see made. Distribute **assessment 21-2**, ask the learners to complete it, and indicate where they can leave the forms as they exit the room.

Thank the participants for their attention, and end with a motivating story, quote, or anecdote from your personal collection.

12:00 p.m.   Adjourn

◆ What to Do Next

- Using the material in this chapter as a guide, build a detailed plan to prepare for this workshop.

- To adjust the length of this session, add more discussion time to the section on team dynamics, to include personalities and team challenges. In addition, you can introduce a project and use it as a recurring example throughout the entire workshop.

- Schedule a training room and invite your attendees. To build interest, include these options: changing the title of the session to a catchy tie-in to your industry or business, sending an introductory email that itemizes common teamwork opportunities in your organization, or doing presentations in individual departmental meetings.

- Draft a supply list, teaching notes, and time estimates. If you'd like to customize your teaching notes, print the slides as note pages and add your own outline to ensure that you don't omit any key points.

- Decide how you will support the action plan to which your learners will commit. If you determine that you want to customize the action plan on **slide 21-21** for your organization, get input from participating department managers on which items they would like to include for action.

- Consider designing follow-up sessions or update emails to encourage each learner to continue to develop his or her teamwork skills.

- For additional modules, background information, and extended training sessions on this subject, refer to the resources used in the development of these materials, specifically *Teamwork Training* by Sharon Boller (ASTD Press, 2005), *Leadership Training* by Lou Russell (ASTD Press, 2003), *Diversity Training* by Cris Wildermuth with Susan Gray (ASTD Press, 2005), and *Innovation Training* by Ruth Ann Hattori and Joyce Wycoff (ASTD Press, 2004).

PowerPoint Slides

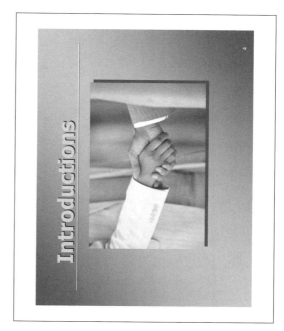

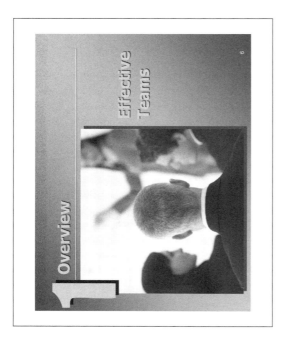

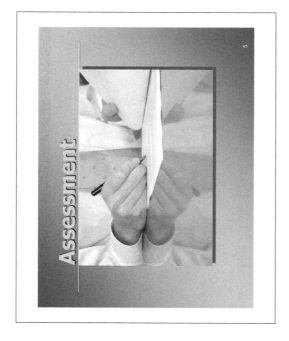

Teamwork Listening Skills

- Ignore distractions
- Good eye contact
- Facial expressions
- Body language
- Ask questions
- Take notes
- Summarize
- Use appropriate responses

14

Team Meetings

- Determine whether a meeting is needed.
- Create a goal for the meeting.
- Send agenda and background information to invitees.
- Set meeting space based on type of meeting.
- Use facilitation procedures.
- Summarize action items, responsibilities, deadlines, and reporting procedures before you adjourn.
- Follow up by sending minutes and monitoring progress.

16

3 Communication in Teams

13

Listening Practice

- Select a partner.
- Identify one of you as the speaker and the other as the listener.
- Speaker talks about a topic of his or her choice for three minutes. Listener uses as many of the teamwork listening skills as possible.
- Listener summarizes discussion.
- Speaker evaluates how listener did.
- Trade roles and repeat.
- Exchange training instruments.

15

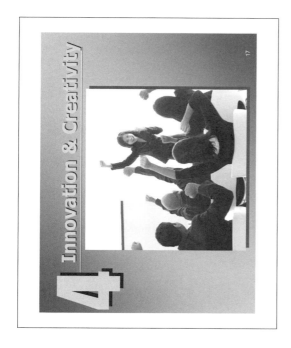

Work-Life Balance

22

What's in This Chapter?

- Objectives for the half-day workshop

- Lists of materials for facilitator and participants

- Detailed program agenda to be used as a facilitator's guide

▲   ▲   ▲

Achieving the proper work-life balance can reduce employee stress, protect against burnout, and create a more fulfilled employee. Businesses can realize the benefits of this balance through reduced sick leave, improved retention rates, and a more productive work force. In this session, learners will have an opportunity to assess their current level of balance, consider their own goals, and assign priorities to their activities to ensure time for both personal and professional development.

The half-day workshop enables attendees to participate in either discussion or practice of the skills of each topic included, and the activities can be adjusted to allow for more in-depth practice, if time is available. At the end of the workshop, learners will commit to action items for continued development.

Training Objectives

The participants' objectives for the half-day workshop are to be able to

- create a balance between personal and business goals and activities

- assign priorities to activities based on desired outcomes and long-term goals

- establish a plan for continued development of a balanced lifestyle.

◎ ✖ Materials

For the facilitator:

- this chapter, for reference and use as a facilitator guide

- Learning Activity 22-1: Introductions

- Learning Activity 22-2: Self-Assessment

  ○ Assessment 22-1: Self-Assessment

- Learning Activity 22-3: Overview

- Learning Activity 22-4: Envisioning Your Ideal Life

  ○ Training Instrument 22-1: Envisioning Your Ideal Life

- Learning Activity 22-5: Breaking for Balance

- Learning Activity 22-6: Focus Areas

  ○ Training Instrument 22-2: Focus Area Mapping Tool

  ○ Training Instrument 22-3: Setting Goals

- Learning Activity 22-7: Distress or De-Stress

- Learning Activity 22-8: Putting It All Together

- Assessment 22-2: Program Evaluation

- PowerPoint slide program, titled "Work-Life Balance" (slides 22-1 through 22-18). To access slides for this program, open the file *UBBB_PowerPointSlides_Ch22.ppt* on the accompanying CD. Thumbnail versions of the slides for this workshop are included at the end of this chapter.

- projector, screen, and computer to display slides

- flipchart and markers.

For the participants:

- pens or pencils for each participant

- name badge for each participant

- set of handouts for each participant

- sticky notes attached to the front of each set of handouts

- assorted toys and puzzles for the participant tables

- snacks and candy as desired.

🕐 Sample Agenda

START	ACTIVITY	MINUTES
:00	Welcome	:05
:05	Objectives and Agenda	:05
:10	Introductions (22-1)	:15
:25	Self-Assessment (22-2)	:20
:45	Overview (22-3)	:20
1:05	Envisioning Your Ideal Life (22-4)	:35
1:40	Breaking for Balance (22-5)	:20
2:00	Break	:15
2:15	Focus Areas (22-6)	:50
3:05	Distress or De-Stress (22-7)	:30
3:35	Putting It All Together (22-8)	:15
3:50	Closing	:10

🕐 8:00 a.m.   Welcome (5 minutes)

PPT As participants enter the room, display **slide 22-1** to greet your learners. Welcome them and introduce yourself. Explain that the purpose of the workshop is to give the learners an opportunity to step away from the rush of daily activities and take time to look at the big picture of their lives. Being effective in their work lives is important, but burnout and overwork are constant threats in today's fast-paced business world. This session will give them tools and techniques to help them maintain a healthy balance in their business and personal lives.

You can expand on this discussion to include specific themes of your organization being addressed by the workshop.

Rules

Explain the ground rules for the session. Here are some sample rules and housekeeping items:

- Turn cell phones to silent. (Turn off your own cell phone first, to lead by example and ensure that your phone isn't the one that rings during the session.)

- This workshop is interactive. The most important things the participants will take away from this class are the ideas and suggestions shared by their fellow learners. They should be prepared to contribute to the discussion. (You can even use small prizes or other incentives to increase participation in the session.)

- A break is scheduled during the session.

- Restrooms, smoking areas, snacks, and vending machines are located in the following areas: *[add details]*.

- Respectful communication is required. If someone is speaking, please give that person your complete attention.

8:05 Objectives and Agenda (5 minutes)

Show **slide 22-2** and review the workshop objectives from the slide. The learners should understand that today's session is designed to help assign priorities and manage activities in all parts of their lives. It will also reduce their stress levels by addressing those areas that are out of balance.

Present the agenda items on **slide 22-3** and ask for questions.

8:10 Introductions (15 minutes)

  Display **slide 22-4** to set the stage for the introductions that will follow. Explain that you would like everyone to meet each other and to think about what work-life balance means to them. Use **learning activity 22-1** to help the learners accomplish this goal.

The next activity will give them a chance to see what areas they can learn more about in today's session.

8:25 Self-Assessment (20 minutes)

Display **slide 22-5**, which introduces the learners to the self-assessment that follows. Use **learning activity 22-2** to help participants assess their areas of strength and potential development as they assign priorities and balance their personal and professional activities.

8:45 Overview (20 minutes)

Present **slide 22-6** as an introduction to the overview. What do we mean by the phrase "work-life balance"? Participants will be able to define this term after they complete **learning activity 22-3** and see **slide 22-7**.

9:05 Envisioning Your Ideal Life (35 minutes)

  It's difficult to picture what's involved in maintaining a balanced lifestyle if you haven't taken the time to imagine what that life would be like. Show **slide 22-8**, which will introduce an opportunity for participants to think about what they like and don't like. Conduct **learning activity 22-4**, in which participants will determine their goals in the development of work-life balance.

9:40   Breaking for Balance (20 minutes)

Conduct **learning activity 22-5** to help learners remember what a break from their day's activities can do for them. This will help them schedule breaks in their work so they can be more productive. After our break, we will learn more about setting goals.

 10:00   Break (15 minutes)

 10:15   Focus Areas (50 minutes)

 Setting goals (**slide 22-9**) in work and personal life is a large part of the planning process. The learners will get a chance to dig deeper into goal setting as you conduct **learning activity 22-6**. This activity, together with **slides 22-10 through 22-12**, helps the participants group their interests into areas of personal focus and professional focus. This allows them to get a more accurate picture of the demands on their time.

 11:05   Distress or De-Stress (30 minutes)

 Despite all the best plans to work on the positive focus areas and reduce the negatives, the world will intrude and create stress, as introduced by **slide 22-13**. The concept to keep in mind about stress is that it will occur, but it's how we decide to handle it that makes all the difference. Use **learning activity 22-7** and **slide 22-14** to help the learners brainstorm methods for stress relief and to keep difficult situations in perspective.

 11:35   Putting It All Together (15 minutes)

 Show **slide 22-15** to indicate that it's time to use all the information imparted during this workshop. Remind the learners that no learning experience is successful without the commitment to an action plan that will put the information to use. Conduct **learning activity 22-8** with **slides 22-16 and 22-17** to create a plan that will continue to develop ways to work toward work-life balance.

 11:50   Closing (10 minutes)

 Present **slide 22-18** at the end of the workshop and remind the participants that your contact information is listed on the slide in case they come up with additional questions when they return to the workplace.

Close the session with a brief discussion of how balance in one's life can have a positive affect on performance in the workplace. Suggest that the learners consider how work-life balance might affect their lives outside the office. Ask them which of the tools they picked up today will help them understand the importance of balance and in what ways they can create a more balanced lifestyle. These are the insights you'd like them to remember as they go back to their departments.

Remind the participants that you, too, want to continue to develop your skills and that they can help you by filling out an evaluation form to let you know what they liked about the session or what changes they would like to see. Distribute **assessment 22-2**, ask the learners complete it, and indicate where to leave the forms when they exit the room.

Thank the learners for their attention and end with a motivating story, quote, or anecdote from your personal collection.

12:00 p.m.   Adjourn

What to Do Next

- Using the material in this chapter as a guide, build a detailed plan to prepare for this workshop.

- To adjust the length of this session, add more discussion time to the section on the art of planning to include specific challenges to a balanced lifestyle. In addition, a section of brainstorming on specific answers to their biggest time-wasters can add a lively activity between some of the more serious planning activities.

- Schedule a training room and invite your attendees. To build interest, you can change the title of the session to a catchy tie-in to your industry or business, send an introductory email that discusses the importance of work-life balance, or do presentations in individual departmental meetings.

- Draft a supply list, teaching notes, and time estimates. If you'd like to customize your teaching notes, print the slides as note pages and add your own outline to ensure that you don't omit key points.

- Decide how you will support the action plan your learners will commit to. If you decide to customize the action plan on **slide 22-17** for your organization, get input from participating department managers on the items they would like to include for action.

- Consider designing follow-up sessions, or update emails to encourage each learner to continue to develop his or her prioritization and life-management skills.

- For additional modules, background information, and extended training sessions on this subject, refer to the resources used in the development of these materials, specifically *Infoline* No. 250408 *"Fundamentals of Work-Life Balance"* by Erica D. Chick (ASTD Press, August 2004) and *Innovation Training* by Ruth Ann Hattori and Joyce Wycoff (ASTD Press, 2004).

PowerPoint Slides

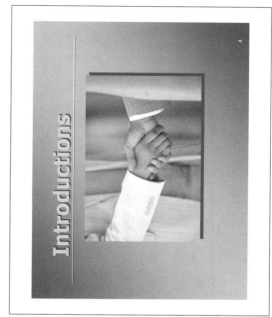

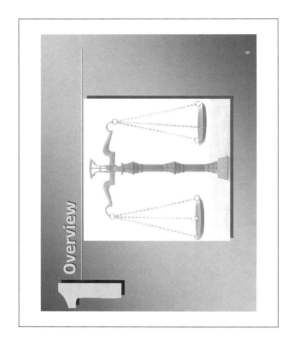

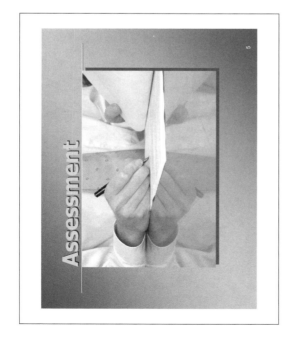

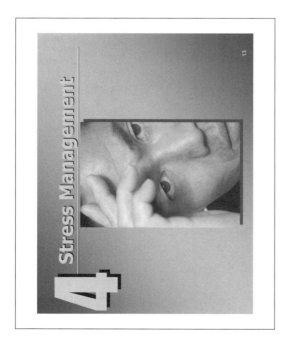

Professional Development 23

What's in This Chapter?

- Objectives for the half-day workshop
- Lists of materials for facilitator and participants
- Detailed program agenda to be used as a facilitator's guide

▲   ▲   ▲

This module on professional development encourages employees to assess their current skill levels, determine their own career map, and set goals and create action plans based on the competencies needed to achieve those goals. At the end of the session, both the organization and the employee experience the benefits of focusing on professional excellence. The organization has a more motivated and strategic-minded employee. The employee has a more realistic view of the advancement available to him or her, as well as a plan to achieve that higher level within the organization.

The half-day workshop enables attendees to participate in either discussion or practice of professional development skills, and the exercises can be adjusted to allow more in-depth practice if time is available. At the end of the workshop, learners will commit to action items for continued development.

Training Objectives

The participants' objectives for the half-day workshop are to be able to

- determine career goals and assess areas for development to achieve those goals
- create a plan for development of professional skills.

◎ ✖ Materials

For the facilitator:

- this chapter, for reference and use as a facilitator guide
- Learning Activity 23-1: Introductions
- Learning Activity 23-2: Self-Assessment
  - Assessment 23-1: Self-Assessment
- Learning Activity 23-3: Overview
- Learning Activity 23-4: Defining Success
  - Training Instrument 23-1: Defining Success
- Learning Activity 23-5: Identifying Skills
  - Training Instrument 23-2: Career and Organizational Success Skills Inventory
  - Training Instrument 23-3: Job Skills and Behavioral Skills Inventory
- Learning Activity 23-6: Resources for Development
  - Training Instrument 23-4: Development Resources
- Learning Activity 23-7: Relationships and Networks
  - Training Instrument 23-5: Relationships and Networks
- Learning Activity 23-8: Development Plan
  - Training Instrument 23-6: Development Plan
- Learning Activity 23-9: Putting It All Together
- Assessment 23-2: Program Evaluation
- PowerPoint slide program, titled "Professional Development" (slides 23-1 through 23-23). To access slides for this program, open the file *UBBB_PowerPointSlides_Ch23.ppt* on the accompanying CD. Thumbnail versions of the slides for this workshop are included at the end of this chapter.
- projector, screen, and computer to display slides
- flipchart and markers.

For the participants:

- pens or pencils for each participant
- name badge for each participant

- set of handouts for each participant
- sticky notes attached to the front of each set of handouts
- assorted toys and puzzles for the participant tables
- snacks and candy as desired.

 ## Sample Agenda

START	ACTIVITY	MINUTES
:00	Welcome	:05
:05	Objectives and Agenda	:05
:10	Introductions (23-1)	:15
:25	Self-Assessment (23-2)	:20
:45	Overview (23-3)	:15
1:00	Define Success (23-4)	:30
1:30	Identifying Skills (23-5)	:30
2:00	Break	:15
2:15	Resources for Development (23-6)	:25
2:40	Relationships and Networks (23-7)	:20
3:00	Development Plan (23-8)	:35
3:35	Putting It All Together (22-9)	:15
3:50	Closing	:10

 ## 8:00 a.m.　Welcome (5 minutes)

PPT　As participants enter the room, display **slide 23-1** as a greeting. Welcome the attendees and introduce yourself. Explain the purpose of the workshop: to give them an opportunity to step away from the rush of daily activities and take time to look at their professional development goals. (You can expand on this discussion to include specific organizational themes being addressed by the workshop.)

Rules

Explain the ground rules for the session. Here are some sample rules and housekeeping items:

- Turn cell phones to silent. (Turn off your own cell phone first, to lead by example and ensure that your phone isn't the one that rings during the session.)

- This workshop is interactive. The most important things that the participants will learn from this class are the ideas and suggestions shared by their fellow learners. They should be prepared to contribute to the discussions. (You can even use small prizes or other incentives to increase participation in the session.)

- A break is scheduled during the session.

- Restrooms, smoking areas, snacks, and vending machines are located in the following areas: *[add details]*.

- Respectful communication is required. If someone is speaking, please give that person your complete attention.

8:05 Objectives and Agenda (5 minutes)

 Show **slide 23-2**. Review the workshop objectives from the slide. The learners should understand that today's session is designed to help them determine their career goals and make a solid plan to develop the areas that will help them move forward toward those objectives.

Go through the agenda items on **slide 23-3**, and ask if the learners have any questions.

8:10 Introductions (15 minutes)

 Show **slide 23-4** to set the stage for the introductions that will follow. Explain that you want everyone to meet each other and think about what professional development means to them. In **learning activity 23-1**, the participants will begin to identify different areas of interest in professional development and get a feel for which area would be most beneficial to their careers.

The next activity will give them a chance to see what areas they can learn more about in today's session.

8:25 Self-Assessment (20 minutes)

 Display **slide 23-5** to introduce the concept of assessment. Use **learning activity 23-2** to help participants assess their areas of strength and potential development.

8:45 Overview (15 minutes)

Congratulate the learners for thinking strategically and deciding to attend a session on professional development. Show **slide 23-6** and use **learning activity 23-3** to give the participants an introduction to the concepts of professional development.

9:00 Define Success (30 minutes)

 Before they start to work on the individual activities of their professional development plan today, the participants need to create a vision of what they're working toward. The way to do that is to think about what they would like to accomplish. Show **slide 23-7** and note that the next activity will help the learners define what success means to them. Conduct **learning activity 23-4** and use **slide 23-8** to determine their goals in professional development.

 9:30   Identifying Skills (30 minutes)

Show **slide 23-9** to prepare participants to identify the skills they need for success and which ones they need to develop. In **learning activity 23-5**, participants will be able to determine the knowledge, skills, and abilities they need for the development and career advancement they hope to achieve.

 10:00   Break (15 minutes)

 10:15   Resources for Development (25 minutes)

Show **slides 23-16** to introduce participants to the steps in plan development. Conduct **learning activity 23-6** with **slide 23-17** to allow participants to determine where they can get information and learn how to develop the skills they need to move forward in their career.

They don't have to go through this process alone, as the next activity shows. They will discover ideas for developing relationships, networks, and mentoring opportunities.

 10:40   Relationships and Networks (20 minutes)

Present **slide 23-18**, which introduces learners to the concept of developing relationships and networks. **Learning activity 23-7** will give participants some ideas on how to develop relationships, networks, and mentoring opportunities, as well as where to find mentors.

 11:00   Development Plan (35 minutes)

Show **slide 23-19**, which introduces the learner to the concept of creating a development plan. In **learning activity 23-8**, participants have the opportunity to use the information they have learned about developing relationships and networks to help them create their own individualized development plan.

 11:35   Putting It All Together (15 minutes)

Present **slide 23-20** to give the participants the idea that it's time to use all the information from the workshop. Conduct **learning activity 23-9**, with **slides 23-21 and 23-22**, presenting a summary of the workshop objectives and a one-day, one-week, and one-month action plan of follow-up activities.

11:50   Closing (10 minutes)

 Display **slide 23-23** and note that your contact information is listed on the slide in case the participants have additional questions once they return to the workplace. Close the session with a brief discussion of what their new picture of professional development includes. Ask the learners which of the tools they picked up today will help them to work toward professional excellence and what actions they could take today for their professional development. Suggest to the participants that these are the insights you'd like them to remember as they go back to their departments.

 Remind the participants that you want to continue to develop your skills too, and that they can help you by filling out an evaluation form to let you know what they liked about the session or what changes they would like to see. Distribute **assessment 23-2**, ask the learners to complete it, and indicate where to leave the forms when they exit the room.

Thank the learners for their attention and end with a motivating story, quote, or anecdote from your personal collection.

 12:00 p.m.   Adjourn

What to Do Next

- Using the material in this chapter as a guide, build a detailed plan to prepare for this workshop.

- To adjust the length of this session, add more discussion time to the section on setting goals, then include addressing the specific questions and concerns of learners. If your organization uses a specific competency system, a section outlining the system would be an excellent addition to the program. Also, a section on methods to maintain motivation could be added to the planning session.

- Schedule a training room and invite your attendees. To build interest, options may include changing the title of the session to a catchy tie-in to your industry or business, sending an introductory email that includes common customer service concerns in your organization, or doing presentations in individual departmental meetings.

- Draft a supply list, teaching notes, and time estimates. If you'd like to customize your teaching notes, print the slides as note pages and add your own outline, to ensure that you don't omit any key points.

- Decide how you will support the action plan your learners will commit to. If you determine that you want to customize the action plan on **slide 23-22** for your organization, get input from participating department managers about which items they would like action on.

- Consider designing follow-up sessions or update emails to encourage each learner to continue to develop his or her professional skills.

- For additional modules, background information, and extended training sessions on this subject, refer to the resources used in the development of these materials, specifically *Infoline* No. 250501 "Building Career Success Skills" by Theodore Pietrzak and Mike Fraum (ASTD Press, January 2005), *Infoline* No. 250401 "Structured Mentoring" by Susan J. Thomas and Patricia J. Douglas (ASTD Press, April 2000), and *Manager Skills Training* by Christee Gabour Atwood (ASTD Press, 2008).

PowerPoint Slides

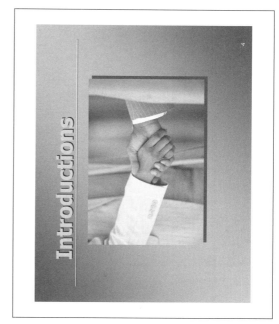

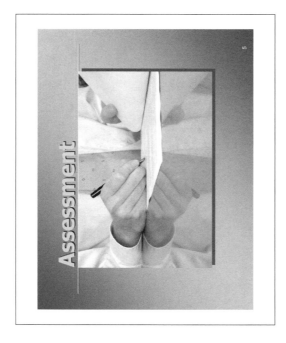

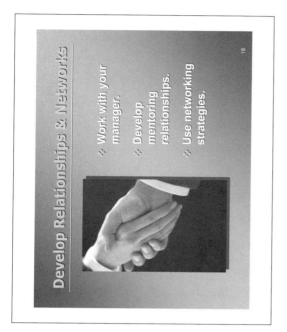

Develop Relationships & Networks

- Work with your manager.
- Develop mentoring relationships.
- Use networking strategies.

18

Putting It All Together

5

20

Determine Development Resources

- What resources could help you learn more about those specific skills?
- How can you connect with those resources?

17

Create Development Plan

- Select methods of development.
- Determine timeline.
- Complete IDP form.
- Enlist support.

19

Action Plan

24 Hours:
Review and make any revisions to your definition of success.

7 Days:
Complete your Individual Development Plan.

30 Days:
Hold an initial interview with a potential mentor.

22

Professional Development

Contact Info

Name of Organization

23

Summary

Our objectives today were to learn to

* determine career goals
* assess areas for development to achieve those goals
* create a plan for development of professional skills.

21

Appendix—Using the Accompanying Compact Disc

Using the Compact Disc—General

Contents of the Compact Disc

You will find these handouts and other tools and support material masters referenced throughout this workbook on the accompanying CD:

- PowerPoint slides

- Learning activities

- Tools

- Assessments

- Training instruments

To access any of these files, insert the CD and click on the appropriate file name.

Computer Requirements

All of the files can be used on a variety of computer platforms.

To read or print the .pdf files included on the CD, Adobe Acrobat Reader software must be installed on your system. This program can be downloaded free of cost from the Adobe website, www.adobe .com.

To use or adapt the contents of the PowerPoint presentation files on the CD, Microsoft PowerPoint software must be installed on your system. If you just want to view the PowerPoint documents, you must have an appropriate viewer installed on your system. Microsoft provides downloads of various viewers free of charge on its website, www.microsoft.com.

Printing From the CD

To print the materials for your sessions, follow these steps:

1. Insert the CD into your computer. Your computer should automatically open up a Windows Explorer window that displays a list of all files on the CD.

2. Locate the handout, PowerPoint file, tool, or support material master you are looking for and double click on the file to open it. If the file you are opening is in .pdf format, the document will open using Adobe Acrobat software. If the file you are opening uses the .ppt format, the document will open in Microsoft PowerPoint. If the file you are opening uses the .doc format, the document will open in Microsoft Word.

3. Print the page or pages of the document(s) that you need for the activity and session.

4. You can print the presentation slides directly from the website using Microsoft PowerPoint. Just open the .ppt files and print as many copies as you need. You can also make handouts of the presentations by printing 2, 4, or 6 slides per page. These slides will be in color, with design elements embedded. PowerPoint also permits you to print these in grayscale or black-and-white representations. Many trainers who use personal computers to project their presentations bring along viewgraphs, just in case there are glitches in the system.

 ## PowerPoint Presentations

The PowerPoint Slides

The PowerPoint presentation slides required for the business skills program or the topic-specific chapters are located on the CD as .ppt files. (They are also included at the end of Chapters 4–23, with their respective chapters.) Each slide is double-numbered by chapter, according to the order in which it appears. You can access individual slides by opening the PowerPoint presentations for the specific topic of interest.

Adapting the PowerPoint Slides

You may find it useful to modify or otherwise customize the slides by opening and editing them in the appropriate application. You must, however, retain the denotation of the original source of the material; it is illegal to pass it off as your own work. You may indicate that a document was adapted from this workbook, written by Christee Gabour Atwood and copyrighted by ASTD. The files will open as "Read Only," so before you adapt them, save them onto your hard drive under a different filename.

Showing the PowerPoint Slides

The following PowerPoint presentations are included on the CD:

Chapter 4 – Basics of Customer Service (slides 4-1 through 4-21)
Chapter 5 – Telephone Skills Training (slides 5-1 through 5-21)
Chapter 6 – Dealing With Difficult Customers (slides 6-1 through 6-21)

Chapter 7 – Internal Customer Service (slides 7-1 through 7-18)
Chapter 9 – Communication Skills (slides 9-1 through 9-37)
Chapter 10 – Presentation Skills (slides 10-1 through 10-20)
Chapter 11 – Basic Networking (slides 11-1 through 11-30)
Chapter 12 – Conflict Management (slides 12-1 through 12-34)
Chapter 14 – Priority Management (slides 14-1 through 14-41)
Chapter 15 – Decision Making and Problem Solving (slides 15-1 through 15-30)
Chapter 16 – Business Writing and Email (slides 16-1 through 16-47)
Chapter 17 – Basic Business Knowledge (slides 17-1 through 17-21)
Chapter 19 – Professional Image (slides 19-1 through 19-21)
Chapter 20 – Social Skills and Basic Etiquette (slides 20-1 through 20-32)
Chapter 21 – Working In Teams (slides 21-1 through 21-22)
Chapter 22 – Work-Life Balance (slides 22-1 through 22-18)
Chapter 23 – Professional Development (slides 23-1 through 23-23).

The presentations are in .ppt format, which means that they will automatically show full screen when you double click on the filename. You can also open Microsoft PowerPoint and launch them from there.

Use the space bar, the enter key, or mouse clicks to advance through a presentation. Press the backspace key to back up. Use the escape key to exit a presentation. If you want to blank the screen to black as the group discusses a point, press the B key. Press it again to restore the show. If you want to blank the screen to a white background, do the same with the W key. Table A-1 summarizes these instructions.

Table A-1. Navigating Through a PowerPoint Presentation

KEY	POWERPOINT "SHOW" ACTION
Space bar *or* Enter *or* Mouse click	Advance through custom animations embedded in the presentation.
Backspace	Back up to the last projected element of the presentation.
Escape	Abort the presentation.
B *or* b B *or* b *(repeat)*	Blank the screen to black. Resume the presentation.
W *or* w W *or* w *(repeat)*	Blank the screen to white. Resume the presentation.

Practice with the slides before you use them to conduct a workshop. You should be able to expand on the content confidently. If you want to engage your training participants fully (rather than worry about how to show the next slide), become familiar with this simple technology before you need to use it. A good practice is to insert notes into the Speaker's Notes feature of the PowerPoint program, print them out, and have them in front of you when you present the slides.

Learning Activities

Learning activities are structured exercises for use in your training session. The types of activities range from self-assessments to role plays to icebreakers. Learning activities often make use of the assessments and training instruments also included on the CD (see sample, p. 271).

These learning activities are available on the CD:

Chapter 4 – Basics of Customer Service
Learning Activity 4-1: Introductions
Learning Activity 4-2: Self-Assessment
Learning Activity 4-3: Customer Expectations
Learning Activity 4-4: Who Are Your
  Customers?
Learning Activity 4-5: Customer Orientation
Learning Activity 4-6: Fantastic Service
  Equation
Learning Activity 4-7: Customer Service
  Practice
Learning Activity 4-8: Putting It All Together

Chapter 5 – Telephone Skills Training
Learning Activity 5-1: Introductions
Learning Activity 5-2: Self-Assessment
Learning Activity 5-3: What's Wrong With
  This Call?
Learning Activity 5-4: The Tone of
  Professionalism
Learning Activity 5-5: Telephone Body Language
Learning Activity 5-6: Telephone Professionalism
Learning Activity 5-7: Telephone Procedures
Learning Activity 5-8: Telephone Challenges
Learning Activity 5-9: Putting It All Together

Chapter 6 – Dealing With Difficult Customers
Learning Activity 6-1: Introductions
Learning Activity 6-2: Self-Assessment
Learning Activity 6-3: Customer Orientation

Learning Activity 6-4: The Difficult Customer
Learning Activity 6-5: The Angry Customer
Learning Activity 6-6: Problem Solving
Learning Activity 6-7: Putting It All Together

Chapter 7 – Internal Customer Service
Learning Activity 7-1: Introductions
Learning Activity 7-2: Self-Assessment
Learning Activity 7-3: Who Are Your Internal
  Customers?
Learning Activity 7-4: Supply and Demand
Learning Activity 7-5: Intake Styles
Learning Activity 7-6: Recognizing and
  Overcoming Communication Challenges
Learning Activity 7-7: Surveying Your Customers
Learning Activity 7-8: Putting It All Together

Chapter 9 – Communication Skills
Learning Activity 9-1: Introductions
Learning Activity 9-2: Self-Assessment
Learning Activity 9-3: The Listening Stick
Learning Activity 9-4: Effective Listening
  Behavior
Learning Activity 9-5: Active Listening Practice
Learning Activity 9-6: Red Flags
Learning Activity 9-7: Body Language
Learning Activity 9-8: Tone Exercise
Learning Activity 9-9: Interpersonal Skills
  Practice
Learning Activity 9-10: Putting It All Together

(SAMPLE) Learning Activity 5-4. The Tone of Professionalism

 OBJECTIVES

The objective of this learning activity is to
- determine the importance of tone in telephone communications.

 MATERIALS

For this activity, you will need
- flipchart and markers.

TIME
- 10 minutes

 INSTRUCTIONS

1. Ask the group to come up with a standard statement that they might say frequently to customers. This could be a simple greeting or a closing to their regular phone calls, such as "Thank you for calling and have a great day."
2. Write this statement on the flipchart page.
3. Note that this seems like a very positive thing to say to customers or to anyone they talk to on the phone. The challenge, however, comes from the fact that we say it during very different experiences.
4. Ask the participants to think of the kinds of emotions and situations a person might experience in an average workday. Give them ideas such as rushed, excited, tired, sarcastic, or happy. List these on the flipchart page.
5. Ask for volunteers to help you by reading the same statement with some of the different emotions listed on the flipchart page. Choose varying emotions so the difference is more obvious.
6. Conduct a debriefing session, using the questions provided.

DISCUSSION QUESTIONS FOR DEBRIEFING

- Could you tell a difference in the way each of these was said?
- Do you sometimes have trouble hiding these emotions in your tone?
- What could you do to be sure that negative emotions aren't reflected in your communications?
- What can we realize from this activity?

Chapter 10 – Presentation Skills

Learning Activity 10-1: Introductions
Learning Activity 10-2: Self-Assessment
Learning Activity 10-3: Overview
Learning Activity 10-4: Writing Your
  Presentation
Learning Activity 10-5: Delivering Your
  Presentation
Learning Activity 10-6: Group Practice Session
Learning Activity 10-7: Putting It All Together

Chapter 11 – Basic Networking

Learning Activity 11-1: Introductions
Learning Activity 11-2: Self-Assessment
Learning Activity 11-3: Networking Overview
Learning Activity 11-4: Building Rapport
Learning Activity 11-5: Creating Partnerships
Learning Activity 11-6: Putting It All Together

Chapter 12 – Conflict Management

Learning Activity 12-1: Introductions
Learning Activity 12-2: Self-Assessment
Learning Activity 12-3: An Overview of Conflict
Learning Activity 12-4: 10 Questions About
  Conflict
Learning Activity 12-5: Personalities in Conflict
Learning Activity 12-6: Resolving Conflict
Learning Activity 12-7: Figuring Things Out
Learning Activity 12-8: Putting It All Together

Chapter 14 – Priority Management

Learning Activity 14-1: Introductions
Learning Activity 14-2: Self-Assessment
Learning Activity 14-3: Mastering Your Time
Learning Activity 14-4: Time Management
  Practice
Learning Activity 14-5: Project Management
Learning Activity 14-6: Managing Records
Learning Activity 14-7: Problem Paper
Learning Activity 14-8: Putting It All Together

Chapter 15 – Decision Making and Problem Solving

Learning Activity 15-1: Introductions
Learning Activity 15-2: Self-Assessment
Learning Activity 15-3: The Five D's of Decision
  Making
Learning Activity 15-4: Decision-Making Practice
Learning Activity 15-5: Problem Solving
Learning Activity 15-6: STEM–System, Training,
  Environment, and Motivation
Learning Activity 15-7: Problem-Solving Activity
Learning Activity 15-8: Putting It All Together

Chapter 16 – Business Writing and Email

Learning Activity 16-1: Introductions
Learning Activity 16-2: Business Writing
  Checkup
Learning Activity 16-3: Business Writing
  Overview
Learning Activity 16-4: Organization of
  Documents
Learning Activity 16-5: Grammar and Tone
Learning Activity 16-6: Email Guidelines
Learning Activity 16-7: Frequently Used
  Documents
Learning Activity 16-8: Putting It All Together

Chapter 17 – Basic Business Knowledge

Learning Activity 17-1: Introductions
Learning Activity 17-2: Self-Assessment
Learning Activity 17-3: Company Overview
Learning Activity 17-4: Basic Business
  Knowledge
Learning Activity 17-5: Business Financials
Learning Activity 17-6: Business Operations
Learning Activity 17-7: Putting It All Together

Chapter 19 – Professional Image

Learning Activity 19-1: Introductions
Learning Activity 19-2: Self-Assessment

Tools

Tools identify items that offer information that participants will find useful in the training session and on the job. There is one tool used in this book, and it can be used as a job aid for providing great customer service (see sample, p. 274).

(SAMPLE) Tool 1. Fantastic Service Equation

1. GREETING THE CUSTOMER	Responsive service starts with a responsive greeting. You only get one first chance to impress a customer, and that first chance lasts only a matter of seconds. Customers expect a friendly greeting, complete with eye contact, a smile, and receptive body language. It's basic. A greeting recognizes a person's worth right off the bat and establishes rapport. A proper greeting immediately says, "I'm here to serve," which is what service is all about. Greetings come in all forms. A parking lot attendant might say, "Glad to see you today." A security guard might open the door for you in the morning, walk you to the elevator, and push the button for your floor. The librarian greets you when he or she says "hello" and smiles before you do, and the customer service representative greets you when he or she answers the phone with a smile and says, "How can I help you today?"
2. DETERMINING NEEDS	The rest of the interaction is determined by the customer's needs. It is fundamental to this part of the equation to listen and ask questions. Listening can help with sales, customer concerns, and problem solving. Proactive listening is the key ingredient to provide responsive, empathic service. When you listen, give the customer your undivided attention and respect. Proactive listening involves total concentration, paraphrasing, and understanding thoughts and feelings—working together with the customer for everyone's benefit.
3. MEETING NEEDS	Once you have determined the customer's needs, it's time to act. An effective response includes acting quickly and with confidence, as well as figuring out what you can do to make the customer happy. It requires giving the customer what was promised, finding out information, delivering a product or service on time, being available to answer a question or answer the phone, and guiding the customer toward a solution.
4. MAKING THE MOMENT MEMORABLE	Here's where your creativity comes into play. This is where you do something special. It could be something big or something little. Whatever it is, it makes the customer feel good. You can create a memorable moment simply by walking a customer to the destination rather than pointing or telling him or her where to go. It could be staying after hours to complete a transaction. It could be following up with a customer to see if the solution you agreed on worked. It could be checking the installation of the equipment you sold. There are many great stories of memorable moments. We all have them. Some of them are grapevine stories that have become customer service folklore—legends passed on from generation to generation of customer service advocates. Consider this one: Nordstrom, a department store that is well known for outstanding service, once had a disgruntled customer come in with a defective tire. The store gladly took back the tire and refunded the customer's money. What's so unusual about this story? Nordstrom doesn't sell tires.
5. CHECKING RESULTS	There is an easy way to see whether you are giving fantastic service: Just ask. Companies and organizations spend a lot of money on surveys, comment cards, and other ways to solicit customer feedback. The frontline workers can be the first to get feedback just by asking, "How was our service today?" Even asking with sincerity, "Is there anything else we can do for you?" is a way to see whether all the customer's needs have been met. You can promote other services when you check results. You can offer the option of another service, or you can tell a customer something he or she didn't know about your organization. Checking results helps solidify the relationship with the customer and improves your organization's image in the customer's eyes. Responses may not always be positive. When you ask for their opinions, customers may complain. A complaint, however, is just an opportunity; it points you toward things to make better and ways to improve. You can make a memorable moment when you handle a complaint effectively.

continued on next page

Tool 1. Fantastic Service Equation, *continued*

	Key Point: A complaint is a memorable moment waiting to happen. Research shows that customers who complain and have their complaints resolved satisfactorily are actually more loyal than those who had no problem at all. Involving customers in your organization and asking about their opinions paves the way for customer loyalty.
6. LEAVING THE DOOR OPEN	There are many ways to encourage customers to return to your organization. Customers like to be appreciated. Leaving the door open is a way to say, "Please come back," or "Thanks for your support." It recognizes them and supports their patronage. You might say: • "Thanks for being our guest here." • "Hope you come back to buy your next birthday present." • "Call me personally if you have any more questions." • "I'll be looking forward to seeing you when you come back with the information we talked about."

Adapted from Customer Service Training by Maxine Kamin © ASTD Press. Used with permission.

There is one tool available on the CD:

Chapter 4 – Basics of Customer Service
Tool 4-1: The Fantastic Service Equation

Assessments

Assessments accompany learning activities and can include self-assessments and evaluation forms (see sample, p. 276). Assessments are used as part of the learning activities.

These assessments are available on the CD:

Chapter 4 – Basics of Customer Service
Assessment 4-1: Self-Assessment
Assessment 4-2: Program Evaluation

Chapter 5 – Telephone Skills Training
Assessment 5-1: Self-Assessment
Assessment 5-2: Program Evaluation

Chapter 6 – Dealing With Difficult Customers
Assessment 6-1: Self-Assessment
Assessment 6-2: Program Evaluation

Chapter 7 – Internal Customer Service
Assessment 7-1: Self-Assessment
Assessment 7-2: Program Evaluation

Chapter 9 – Communication Skills
Assessment 9-1: Self-Assessment
Assessment 9-2: Program Evaluation

Chapter 10 – Presentation Skills
Assessment 10-1: Self-Assessment
Assessment 10-2: Program Evaluation

Chapter 11 – Basic Networking
Assessment 11-1: Self-Assessment
Assessment 11-2: Program Evaluation

Chapter 12 – Conflict Management
Assessment 12-1: Self-Assessment
Assessment 12-2: Program Evaluation

Chapter 14 – Priority Management
Assessment 14-1: Self-Assessment
Assessment 14-2: Program Evaluation

Chapter 15 – Decision Making and Problem Solving
Assessment 15-1: Self-Assessment
Assessment 15-2: Program Evaluation

Chapter 16 – Business Writing and Email
Assessment 16-1: Self-Assessment
Assessment 16-2: Program Evaluation

Chapter 17 – Basic Business Knowledge
Assessment 17-1: Self-Assessment
Assessment 17-2: Program Evaluation

Chapter 19 – Professional Image
Assessment 19-1: Self-Assessment
Assessment 19-2: Program Evaluation

Chapter 20 – Social Skills and Basic Etiquette
Assessment 20-1: Self-Assessment
Assessment 20-2: Program Evaluation

Chapter 21 – Working In Teams
Assessment 21-1: Self-Assessment
Assessment 21-2: Program Evaluation

(SAMPLE) Assessment 12-1. Conflict Management Self-Assessment

1 = Never	2 = Seldom	3 = Sometimes	4 = Often	5 = Most of the Time

Next to each behavior listed below, write the number that indicates how frequently you act or respond in these ways.

UNDERSTANDING AND ADDRESSING CONFLICT

1. I recognize the difference between good and bad conflict.   1 2 3 4 5
2. I avoid procrastination by immediately addressing conflict situations.   1 2 3 4 5
3. I actively pursue mutually beneficial outcomes.   1 2 3 4 5
4. I understand the difference between assertive and aggressive.   1 2 3 4 5
5. I enter into conflict negotiations with an open mind.   1 2 3 4 5

Total score for this section ____

MANAGING CONFLICT

6. I seek to determine the source of the conflict by looking beyond symptoms and uncovering the root problem.   1 2 3 4 5
7. I solicit input from all parties involved before I make decisions.   1 2 3 4 5
8. I seek to maintain a positive environment for conflict resolution.   1 2 3 4 5
9. I use fair and consistent guidelines for conflict negotiations.   1 2 3 4 5
10. I remain calm in difficult situations.   1 2 3 4 5

Total score for this section ____

ATTITUDES TOWARD CONFLICT

11. I view conflict as an opportunity to improve and grow.   1 2 3 4 5
12. I accept that, if managed properly, conflict promotes a healthy exchange of ideas and opinions.   1 2 3 4 5
13. I appreciate the different personality types and traits that are represented on my team.   1 2 3 4 5
14. I understand my personal biases and put them aside to think objectively about the situation at hand.   1 2 3 4 5
15. I work to ensure that others are not hesitant to approach me for help with conflict or difficult situations.   1 2 3 4 5

Total score for this section ____

OPPORTUNITIES

16. I address conflict challenges with a positive outlook and consider goals, ethics, and values.   1 2 3 4 5
17. I recognize the benefits of diverse thinking for my team.   1 2 3 4 5
18. I do not make inappropriate comments or use foul language.   1 2 3 4 5
19. I welcome ideas and suggestions for improvement from others at all levels of the organization.   1 2 3 4 5
20. I take the time to review and document lessons learned from conflict management situations.   1 2 3 4 5

Total score for this section ____

Survey TOTAL ____

continued on next page

(SAMPLE) Assessment 12-1. Conflict Management Self-Assessment

1 = Never	2 = Seldom	3 = Sometimes	4 = Often	5 = Most of the Time

Next to each behavior listed below, write the number that indicates how frequently you act or respond in these ways.

UNDERSTANDING AND ADDRESSING CONFLICT

1. I recognize the difference between good and bad conflict.   1 2 3 4 5
2. I avoid procrastination by immediately addressing conflict situations.   1 2 3 4 5
3. I actively pursue mutually beneficial outcomes.   1 2 3 4 5
4. I understand the difference between assertive and aggressive.   1 2 3 4 5
5. I enter into conflict negotiations with an open mind.   1 2 3 4 5

Total score for this section ____

MANAGING CONFLICT

6. I seek to determine the source of the conflict by looking beyond symptoms and uncovering the root problem.   1 2 3 4 5
7. I solicit input from all parties involved before I make decisions.   1 2 3 4 5
8. I seek to maintain a positive environment for conflict resolution.   1 2 3 4 5
9. I use fair and consistent guidelines for conflict negotiations.   1 2 3 4 5
10. I remain calm in difficult situations.   1 2 3 4 5

Total score for this section ____

ATTITUDES TOWARD CONFLICT

11. I view conflict as an opportunity to improve and grow.   1 2 3 4 5
12. I accept that, if managed properly, conflict promotes a healthy exchange of ideas and opinions.   1 2 3 4 5
13. I appreciate the different personality types and traits that are represented on my team.   1 2 3 4 5
14. I understand my personal biases and put them aside to think objectively about the situation at hand.   1 2 3 4 5
15. I work to ensure that others are not hesitant to approach me for help with conflict or difficult situations.   1 2 3 4 5

Total score for this section ____

OPPORTUNITIES

16. I address conflict challenges with a positive outlook and consider goals, ethics, and values.   1 2 3 4 5
17. I recognize the benefits of diverse thinking for my team.   1 2 3 4 5
18. I do not make inappropriate comments or use foul language.   1 2 3 4 5
19. I welcome ideas and suggestions for improvement from others at all levels of the organization.   1 2 3 4 5
20. I take the time to review and document lessons learned from conflict management situations.   1 2 3 4 5

Total score for this section ____

Survey TOTAL ____

continued on next page

Chapter 22 – Work-Life Balance
Assessment 22-1: Self-Assessment
Assessment 22-2: Program Evaluation

Chapter 23 – Professional Development
Assessment 23-1: Self-Assessment
Assessment 23-2: Program Evaluation

 Training Instruments

Training instruments are interactive training materials for participants' use. They include items such as sample phone scripts, checklists, definitions, and more (see sample, p. 278). As with assessments, training instruments are used during learning activities.

These training instruments are available on the CD:

Chapter 4 – Basics of Customer Service
Training Instrument 4-1: Categories of Customer Expectations
Training Instrument 4-2: Who Are Your Customers?
Training Instrument 4-3: Customer Service Practice Exercise
Training Instrument 4-4: Evaluation Checklist

Chapter 5 – Telephone Skills Training
Training Instrument 5-1: What's Wrong With This Call?
Training Instrument 5-2: Telephone Procedures
Training Instrument 5-3: LAST Formula for Challenging Telephone Conversations
Training Instrument 5-4: Practice Situations

Chapter 6 – Dealing With Difficult Customers
Training Instrument 6-1: Techniques for Difficult Customer Situations
Training Instrument 6-2: The Difficult Customer Situation
Training Instrument 6-3: Angry Customer Practice Cards
Training Instrument 6-4: LAST Formula for Difficult Customer Situations
Training Instrument 6-5: Problem-Solving Practice Situations

Chapter 7 – Internal Customer Service
Training Instrument 7-1: Who Are Your Internal Customers?
Training Instrument 7-2: Language System Diagnostic Instrument
Training Instrument 7-3: Recognizing and Overcoming Communication Challenges
Training Instrument 7-4: Internal Customer Service Survey

Chapter 9 – Communication Skills
Training Instrument 9-1: Red Flags
Training Instrument 9-2: Body Language
Training Instrument 9-3: Tone
Training Instrument 9-4: Interpersonal Skills

Chapter 10 – Presentation Skills
Training Instrument 10-1: The SET Formula
Training Instrument 10-2: Presentation Planning Form
Training Instrument 10-3: Presentation Tips
Training Instrument 10-4: Guidelines for Visual Aids

Chapter 11 – Basic Networking
Training Instrument 11-1: Networking Worksheet
Training Instrument 11-2: Planning the Partnership

(SAMPLE) Training Instrument 14-3.   Project Management Chart

Instructions:
- Brainstorm to determine all the steps of your project.
- Place the steps in order in the chart below.
- Estimate how long each action item will take.
- If time is limited, use reverse engineering to determine deadlines by starting with the completion date and then dating each action item from last to first. Remember that other tasks may need to be rescheduled to allow time for completion of this project.
- Adjust completion date if needed to ensure that you are not creating unrealistic goals.
- Assign responsibility for the task.
- Determine any additional resources that can help with this task.
- Notes column is optional. Notes can be recorded on this chart or in project folder.
- Tracking symbols include: ✓ Complete × Delete *IP* In Progress

Project Management Chart

TRACKING	ACTION	DEADLINE	RESPONSIBLE	RESOURCES	NOTES
Symbols: ✓ Complete × Delete *IP* In Progress	*Always starts with a verb.*	*Must be completed by…*	*Who will do this?*	*What is needed? What can help with this task?*	*What needs to happen first? Other notes.*

For Further Reading

Appleman, J. *10 Steps to Successful Business Writing.* Alexandria, Virginia: ASTD Press, 2008.

Atwood, C. G. *Manager Skills Training.* Alexandria, Virginia: ASTD Press, 2008.

Atwood, C. G. *Presentation Skills Training.* Alexandria, Virginia: ASTD Press, 2007.

Boller, S. *Teamwork Training.* Alexandria, Virginia: ASTD Press, 2005.

Cherniss, C., and M. Adler. *Promoting Emotional Intelligence in Organizations.* Alexandria, Virginia: ASTD Press, 2000.

Chick, E. D. *Fundamentals of Work-Life Balance.* Alexandria, Virginia: ASTD Infoline, 2004.

Downs, L. J. *Listening Skills Training.* Alexandria, Virginia: ASTD Press, 2008.

Downs, L. J. *Time Management Training.* Alexandria, Virginia: ASTD Press, 2008.

Emily Post Institute, *http://www.emilypost.com*, 2009.

Eyring, P. *Mind Your Business Manners.* Alexandria, Virginia: ASTD Infoline, 2008

Feldman, J., and K. Mulle. *Put Emotional Intelligence to Work.* Alexandria, Virginia: ASTD Press, 2007.

Haneberg, L. *Developing Great Managers.* Alexandria, Virginia: ASTD Press, 2008.

Hattori, R. A., and J. Wycoff. *Innovation Training.* Alexandria, Virginia: ASTD Press, 2004.

Kamin, M. *Customer Service Training.* Alexandria, Virginia: ASTD Press, 2002.

Kaye, B. P., and D. Scheef. *Mentoring.* Alexandria, Virginia: ASTD Infoline (no. 0004), April 2000.

Mikula, J. *Sales Training.* Alexandria, Virginia: ASTD Press, 2003.

Orey, M., and J. Prisk. *Communication Skills Training.* Alexandria, Virginia: ASTD Press, 2004.

Pietrzak, T. P., and M. Fraum. *Building Career Success Skills.* Alexandria, Virginia: ASTD Infoline, January 2005.

Protocol School of Washington, *http://www.psow.com* (n.d.).

Russell, L. *Leadership Training.* Alexandria, Virginia: ASTD Press, 2003.

Shackelford, B. *Project Management Training.* Alexandria, Virginia: ASTD Press, 2004.

Thomas, Susan P., and P. J. Douglas. *Structured Mentoring.* Alexandria, Virginia: ASTD Infoline, April 2000.

Van Tiem, D. P., and J. M. Rosenzweig, *Performance Excellence Through Partnering.* Alexandria, Virginia: ASTD Infoline (no. 250504), April 2005.

Wildermuth, C., and S. Gray. *Diversity Training.* Alexandria, Virginia: ASTD Press, 2005.

About the Author

Christee Gabour Atwood is a speaker and facilitator whose mission statement is "Linking Laughter and Learning." Her goal is to help individuals communicate and share their wisdom. Christee has worked with groups ranging from corporations and associations, community organizations, and work-release programs to city and state government agencies, to develop and present programs that develop communication skills.

Recipient of the 2006 Outstanding Adjunct Faculty Award at Baton Rouge Community College, Atwood has been a radio personality, television host and anchor, and newspaper and magazine columnist. She has also served as executive director for state associations, editor and publisher of various trade and professional magazines, and CEO of The Communications Workshop, Inc.

Atwood is a master facilitator for the Small Business Training Center in Baton Rouge, Louisiana, and has received training certifications from various organizations, including Franklin Covey and AchieveGlobal. Her published works include the humorous book *Three Feet Under: Journal of a Midlife Crisis*. *Ultimate Basic Business Skills: Training an Effective Workforce* is Atwood's fifth book with ASTD Press. Her other ASTD Press titles are *Succession Planning* (2007), *Presentation Skills Training* (2008), *Manager Skills Training* (2008), and *Knowledge Management Basics* (2009). She can be reached at www.christee.biz.

Index

A

Accountability in Difficult Situations *(Training Instrument 19-2),* 204, 279

Accountability of Professionals *(Learning Activity 19-5),* 204, 206, 273

Active Listening Practice *(Learning Activity 9-5),* 74, 77, 270

Angry Customer, The *(Learning Activity 6-5),* 46, 49, 270

Angry Customer Practice Cards *(Training Instrument 6-3),* 46, 277

Assessment 4-1: Self-Assessment, 20, 275

Assessment 4-2: Program Evaluation, 20, 24, 275

Assessment 5-1: Self-Assessment, 32, 275

Assessment 5-2: Program Evaluation, 32, 36, 275

Assessment 6-1: Self-Assessment, 46, 275

Assessment 6-2: Program Evaluation, 46, 50, 275

Assessment 7-1: Self-Assessment, 58, 275

Assessment 7-2: Program Evaluation, 58, 62, 275

Assessment 9-1: Self-Assessment, 74, 275

Assessment 9-2: Program Evaluation, 74, 78, 275

Assessment 10-1: Self-Assessment, 92, 275

Assessment 10-2: Program Evaluation, 92, 95, 275

Assessment 11-1: Self-Assessment, 104, 275

Assessment 11-2: Program Evaluation, 104, 107, 275

Assessment 12-1: Self-Assessment, 118, 275–276

Assessment 12-2: Program Evaluation, 118, 122, 275

Assessment 14-1: Self-Assessment, 138, 275

Assessment 14-2: Program Evaluation, 138, 141, 275

Assessment 15-1: Self-Assessment, 156, 275

Assessment 15-2: Program Evaluation, 156, 160, 275

Assessment 16-1: Self-Assessment, 170, 275

Assessment 16-2: Program Evaluation, 170, 174, 275

Assessment 17-1: Self-Assessment, 188, 275

Assessment 17-2: Program Evaluation, 188, 192, 275

Assessment 19-1: Self-Assessment, 204, 275

Assessment 19-2: Program Evaluation, 204, 207, 275

Assessment 20-1: Self-Assessment, 216, 275

Assessment 20-2: Program Evaluation, 216, 220, 275

Assessment 21-1: Self-Assessment, 232, 275

Assessment 21-2: Program Evaluation, 232, 236, 275

Assessment 22-1: Self-Assessment, 244, 277

Assessment 22-2: Program Evaluation, 244, 248, 277

Assessment 23-1: Self-Assessment, 256, 277

Assessment 23-2: Program Evaluation, 256, 260, 277

Attitude of Professionalism, The *(Learning Activity 19-4),* 204, 206, 273

B

balance between work, life, 243–253
  adjournment, 248
  agenda, 245–248
  breaks, 247
  closing, 247–248
  distress, 247
  focus areas, 247
  ideal life, envisioning of, 246
  introductions, 246
  materials, 244
  objectives, 246
  overview, 246
  PowerPoint slides, 245–253
  self-assessment, 246
  training objectives, 243
  welcome, 245–246

Basic Business Knowledge *(Learning Activity 17-4),* 188, 191, 272

Basic Business Knowledge *(Training Instrument 17-3),* 188, 279

basic business skills, 133–198

"Basic Business Knowledge" (slides 17-1 through 17-21), PowerPoint slide program, 188

"Basic Networking" (slides 11-1 through 11-30), PowerPoint slide program, 104

"Basics of Customer Service" (slides 4-1 through 4-21), PowerPoint slide program, 20

Body Language *(Learning Activity 9-7),* 74, 77, 270

285